RED LETTER
REVOLUTION

red letter revolution.

if we did revolutions Jesus' way...

Colin McCartney

foreword by Larry N. Willard

Red Letter Revolution: If We Did Revolution Jesus' Way

Copyright ©2009 Colin McCartney
All rights reserved
Printed in Canada
International Standard Book Number: 978-1-894860-41-3

Published by:
Castle Quay Books
1-1295 Wharf Street, Pickering, Ontario, L1W 1A2
Tel: (416) 573-3249   Fax: (416) 981-7922
E-mail: info@castlequaybooks.com
www.castlequaybooks.com

Copy editing by Marina H. Hofman
Printed at Essence Printing, Belleville, Ontario

Library and Archives Canada Cataloguing in Publication

McCartney, Colin, 1964-

Red letter revolution / Colin McCartney; foreword, Larry N. Willard.

Includes bibliographical references.
ISBN 978-1-894860-41-3

1. Jesus Christ--Teachings. I. Title.

BS2415.M33 2009   232   C2009-901602-8

CASTLE QUAY BOOKS

CONTENTS

ACKNOWLEDGEMENTS

Attempting to live out Jesus' Red Letter Revolution is no easy task. This is why I am so thankful for the following people who walk with me along the revolutionary path of Jesus.

First and foremost, I thank my wife for her incredible support, love and wisdom. Your prayers, encouragement and generous spirit are the wind beneath my wings. You are my biggest blessing and best comrade in arms. To my children, C.J. and Victoria, you make the world I live in more like the kingdom of God because of your presence in my life. To my mother and father: Dad, you are enjoying the fruits of the revolution with our heavenly Father. Mom, thanks for your support and forgive me for what I wrote about the Irish (though it is all true)!

Thanks to Brett and Stephanie McBride and your team of crazy revolutionaries at UrbanPromise Toronto. You are all precious to me, and I wish I could mention all of you by name. Know that I love and appreciate every one of you. To Bill and Gail Masson, Joe and Lois Tullo, the D.E. boys and your families, Victor and Stacy Abuharoon, the Jungs and my good Irish troublemaker friend, John McAuley—all of you have a special place in my heart. To the Horwoods—your cottage was a special oasis for me to write this book. To Tony Campolo and the rest of our Red Letter gang—let us keep the fire burning. To all my other brothers and sisters in arms at UrbanPromise International, Youth Unlimited, Yonge Street Mission and World Vision Canada—you are all a great inspiration!

To the Castle Quay Books family and especially the ever patient Larry Willard and Marina H. Hofman: we are done! No more late nights and early mornings. This book could not have happened without you.

Finally, to all those who suffer injustice in our world today: forgive me for my part in your sufferings. You are not forgotten. Jesus walks with you and is raising up a movement of Red Letter Christians who will speak for the voiceless and act on behalf of the weak. Your resurrection is coming. Blessed are they who come in the name of the Lord!

FOREWORD

Colin McCartney writes like a man with a divine mission and a fire to see it accomplished. It is understandable, since he has worked with the broken souls of our city for years and sees a need so deep and vast that he understands only God himself can fill it.

But he also knows that God almost exclusively works through his "called" people. In *Red Letter Revolution*, Colin reminds us that as followers of Christ we have been commissioned to deny ourselves and focus on completing the work of Jesus as our top priority. Colin senses that the service of too many Christians is divided and lacks luster. He knows there are ways we could really impact our city, if only we would all pull together, totally dedicated to Christ and focused on his work. Thus, Colin's frustration and excitement are equally displayed here.

In this book, Colin beckons us to become part of a new movement that is already taking shape in nations around the world. It's an army of like-minded women and men resolving to shake the practices of "normal" Christianity. The individuals in this movement are called Red Letter Christians, persons dedicated to model their lives and actions on the words of Jesus as found in many red letter editions of the New Testament. This group of radical believers is not satisfied with the way Christ's church is responding to the Lord's commission, seemingly content to standby as a lost and broken people suffer, helplessly marching into a dark eternity.

Whatever the personal cost, Red Letter Christians want to make an eternal difference in our world. They take their action plan from every recorded word that Jesus spoke and they do exactly what Jesus asks of them. They acknowledge that apart from him they can do nothing. But they know that Christ waits for them to act on his commands so that he can empower them to do something significant for God's glory.

Colin is not an idealist living in an academic cocoon and writing about lofty early church concepts that should be modernized for us. His passion and call to action is energized by what he sees every day in the streets and back alleys of our city; scenes that invade the streets of every other city in our nation. With an eye on the mountain of personal needs of the down-trodden, he is motivated by the words of Jesus to become a hand and voice for the helpless.

He implores you to make a difference in this time of increasing tribulation and trial, where everywhere, everyday, there are hurting people whose hearts are failing them for fear of what is coming upon the whole earth. This group of hurting men and women feel like abandoned souls and need the light and the love of Christ that only you and I can bring.

Colin believes that it is in this present darkness that God's light shines brightest and the true model of Jesus' love works the mightiest. He knows there are people out there at this very moment that are ready to give up all hope. They bear the chains of failure and oppression like an anchor. And he believes you and I are all that separates them from their present darkness and a new life and beginning. But he asks: Will we respond to the call?

In this work, Colin includes a set of historically tried and tested disciplines that he believes will equip the follower of Jesus to respond to these serious demands placed on us. We cannot undertake this role in our own ineffective power. So, Colin presents a formula that includes personal discipline and action and a high dependence on the love and the power of the Spirit that can flow through us to do great things for God. Colin reminds us that in history, these same simple dynamics and principles have fueled everything from the Reformation, great revivals and mission movements to every major spiritual renewal.

The core elements are trust in God, selfless willingness to be obedient to the words of Jesus exactly as they are found in the red letter editions of the scriptures, a command to be filled with the love of God and a heart fully submitted to the Holy Spirit. The principles are faultless and timeless. Like a perfect recipe, when these ingredients are brought together, a supernatural meal results.

As I read Colin's book, I am reminded of stories I have read during seminary training of godly servants who earnestly sought to do the work of Jesus and who regularly followed these principles. The results were amazing. I think of the Haystack movement that started when Samuel J. Mills (1783-1818) and several students at Williams College took refuge from a rainstorm under a haystack one afternoon. While they were waiting for the rain to stop, another rain arrived. The Holy Spirit showed up and led them to start praying for the needs of the lost throughout the world. The were deeply moved and committed themselves at that very prayer meeting to bring the pure gospel overseas to every people the Lord would allow them to reach. That day, a major movement started that grew to become a missions movement powerhouse.

I think of the work of Count Zinzendorf (1700-1760), a simple man who led a group of Moravians to the most significant missions movement of his day. He stated that his primary life motive was to unite fellow believers in Christ's love and bring the compassion of Jesus to the whole lost world. Apart from his many personal successes, he strongly influenced Charles and John Wesley, who followed his model and went on to be credited with endless social improvements during their time in England, helping millions. Some historians have even credited their movement with saving England from a bloody French-style revolution. Because of their love and compassion for the poor, the people of England came to emulate them and a movement of compassion swept that whole empire. As a result, God blessed the entire country.

I could write endlessly about William and Catherine Booth, who practiced the same principals and whose work led to a refocus on sharing the immense wealth generated in the new industrial cities of Europe. The hearts of many were opened, and wealth spread to meet the needs of the poor, resulting in a great spiritual revival. Nearly every important social program in our country today can be traced to the initiatives started by these great servants of Jesus. Could the same occur in our day?

The secret to these great leaders' success is captured perfectly by Colin. They were filled with the love of God and compassion of Christ and obeyed what they understood to be the clearest commands of God, as spoken by Jesus in the Gospels. They understood Jesus' words that people do not live by bread (food) alone, but also need the spiritual bread of the words of God. If this is true, then we need to feed on Jesus' words as essentially as we feed our bodies each day. Jesus called his own words light, bread, life, food and understanding and warned that ignoring his words would have critical and disastrous consequences. How can we ignore something so essential?

Once supernaturally fed, informed by the words of Jesus and clothed with love and the power of the Holy Spirit, our works for God will be most effective. A life fully submitted to Jesus and his cause will have the power needed to respond to poverty, racism, economic disparity, violence, classism, sexism and all other forms of injustice and oppression in our world.

As you read Colin's words, you will find that he challenges a comfortable form of safe, somewhat self-focused, religious Christianity—a version, he argues, Jesus did not design. He asks you to embrace a radical framework for returning to the revolutionary style of life and ministry that Jesus always intended. Should you embrace the calling, be warned that you will likely not become popular with either comfortable Christians or the worldly. This is not the kind of life that delights these groups. But know you will be delighting the heart of God and fulfilling the longing of the heart of Jesus. A longing present since he returned to the throne of his Father and waits for that final command to end the age. I can only imagine that in the halls of justice in heaven eyes are on us, and the discussion concerns the question of whether we will take up this challenge or live out our lives in meaningless ease.

Colin's only question to you is the same one that Jesus is asking: Are you ready and willing to accept the challenge to join the revolution?

INTRODUCTION

Tranquility.

For centuries this was the rule of law that governed the people living in a quaint, old-fashioned French town depicted in the movie *Chocolat*, starring Juliette Binoche and Johnny Depp.[1] Year after year, for centuries on end, the townspeople of this fictional country village went through the motions of a very safe and undisturbed life, never taking risks, never tasting "joie de vivre" and never truly living.

That all changed when the striking Vianne (Binoche) came to town one cold, blustery day. Like the north wind that blew in on the village the day she arrived, she instantly became an unpredictable, strong breath of fresh air to the town. Her arrival caused quite a stir among the people, as she slowly went about the work of establishing an unusual chocolate shop in the heart of the drab village.

Each day, Vianne would splash on colourful paint to brighten up the dark walls of her shop or decorate the countertops with artistic collections taken from all parts of the world.

And, every day, as she livened up her chocolatier, curious townspeople watched her every move. Everything she did was so different, so opposite and extraordinarily freeing compared to what the townspeople were accustomed to. The clothing she wore was colourful, theirs dowdy. Her attitude was jovial, theirs joyless. She symbolized hope, they represented fear. Her stylishly artful shop stood out from all the other monotonous stores that were lined up together on the dreary village streets. She greeted others with a smile on her face, while everyone else seemed to have a permanent frown glued onto their faces. She took genuine interest in the people she met, while everyone else focused on their own personal affairs.

Best of all, she created the most tantalizing, mouth-watering chocolate confections that magically inspired her customers to abandon their lifeless existence to enter a new life of love, risk taking and joy.

This caught the eye of the domineering mayor, who bristled at the changes Vianne introduced to the town, changes that disturbed his definition of tranquility. He opposed her every move, but in the end he was won over by her kindness and grace. The life of tedium that he lived could not withstand the effervescent life she gave, and his way of living was no match for the love, joy and life that oozed from Vianne's very being.

Juliette Binoche's character Vianne was the epitome of life. She was the only beacon of hope in the dreary existence of the townspeople who walked every day in trepidation of disturbing the false tranquility that ruled the village.

To me, she epitomizes what Christians are to be in our world. We are to bring life, excitement, love and grace to a weary world that sorely lacks true life and purpose. In the words of Jesus, we are to be the "salt of the earth" (Mt 5:13), God's people that add zest to life. We are also to be "the light of the world" (Mt 5:14), God's radiant ones who bring his light into darkness through our tantalizing and mouth watering lifestyles. We are the ones who embody Jesus, who brings "life and life to the full" (Jn 10:10).

In a world entrapped by the rules of commercialism and competition that so powerfully suck the life out of everyone under the thumb of materialistic totalitarianism, we are to offer an alternative life, a new way of living the freedom that only the kingdom of God brings.

How can we live like Vianne? How can we experience the freedom and true joy of life that Jesus promises us? And how do we offer this life to a world that sorely lacks it?

This book encourages you to wrestle with these questions and embrace a vibrant way of living known as the Red Letter Revolution of Jesus Christ.

PART ONE

JESUS THE REVOLUTIONARY

"Any man who afflicts the human race with ideas must be prepared to see them misunderstood, and that is what happened to Jesus."

Henry Louis Mencken

"I'm a Muslim, but do you think Jesus would love me? I think Jesus would have a drink with me… He would be cool. He would talk to me. No Christian ever did that. They'd throw me in jail and write bad articles about me and then go to church on Sunday and say Jesus is a wonderful man and he's coming back to save us. But they don't understand that when he comes back, that these crazy greedy capitalistic men are gonna kill him again."

Mike Tyson (former heavyweight champion of the world)

"Christianity alone has felt that God, to be wholly God, must be a rebel as well as a king."

G. K. Chesterton

"If Jesus had been killed 20 years ago, Catholic school children would be wearing little electric chairs around their necks instead of crosses."

Lenny Bruce

"If you're going to follow Jesus, well, he got killed. That's just part of the job description: making trouble for peace."

Dan Berrigan (Jesuit priest, activist)

"Jesus, undeterred, went right ahead and gave his charge: God authorized and commanded me to commission you: Go out and train everyone you meet, far and near, in this way of life, marking them by baptism in the threefold name: Father, Son and Holy Spirit. Then instruct them of all I have commanded you. I'll be with you as you do this, day after day, right up to the end of the age."

Jesus (Mt 28:18-20, *The Message*)

THE REBEL JESUS

The streets are filled with laughter and light
And the music of the season
And the merchants' windows are all bright
With the faces of the children
And the families hurrying to their homes
As the sky darkens and freezes
Will be gathering around their hearths and tables
Giving thanks for God's graces
And the birth of the rebel Jesus

They call him by the "Prince of Peace"
And they call him by "the Saviour"
And they pray to him upon the sea
And in every bold endeavour
And they fill his churches with their pride and gold
As their faith in him increases
But they've turned the nature that I worship in
From a temple to a robber's den
In the words of the rebel Jesus

We guard our world with locks and guns
And we guard our fine possessions
And once a year when Christmas comes
We give to our relations
And perhaps we give a little to the poor
If the generosity should seize us
But if anyone of us should interfere
In the business of why there are poor
They get the same as the rebel Jesus

But pardon me if I have seemed
To take the tone of judgment
For I've no wish to come between
This day and your enjoyment
In a life of hardship and of earthly toil
There's a need for anything that frees us

COLIN MCCARTNEY

So I bid you pleasure and I bid you cheer
From a heathen and a pagan
On the side of the rebel Jesus

Words and music by Jackson Browne (Elektra Entertainment, 1997)

CHAPTER ONE

A Tale of
Two Revolutionaries

"All at once
The world can overwhelm me
There's almost nothing that you could tell me
That could ease my mind
Which way will you run?
When it's always all around you
And the feeling lost and found you again
A feeling that we have no control"

"All at Once," words and music by Jack Johnson
(Brushfire Records, 2008)

For centuries, humanity has longed for a time when war, hunger, sickness and oppression are abolished. But these problems persist, and with the advance of modern technology, we are given a front row seat in watching a global horror show of devastating nightmares. All of this can be overwhelming, paralyzing us from taking action in making our world a better, more just place to live in.

Yet, I still possess an audacity of hope for our world. I believe we can make a difference. I confidently embrace the challenge for change. I boldly declare that in a world filled with injustice, oppression and inequality, it is time for a revolution!

But who can lead such a radical transformation? Who can be a revolutionary leader that can bring about lasting change? The answer is found in a revolutionary who lived long ago. This revolutionary was far different than any other radical.

To illustrate his radical effectiveness, I will compare him with another famous rebel of times past. Though separated by time and circumstance, they had much in common. In fact, their similarities were key components that shaped their fervent message for change. In all probability, they shared the experience of great shame, growing up under the glare of suspicious eyes, having been conceived out of wedlock. They both witnessed great injustice done to their people by greedy and oppressive powers. Experiencing the pain of being a foreigner, they understood the fear of homelessness and the curse of poverty. These shared life circumstances were formative in shaping their strong revolutionary tendencies, filling them with a passion for justice accompanied with grand dreams of a better future for all humanity.

These radicals possessed brilliant minds, matched by incredible oratory skill. Driven by unwavering confidence and empowered by their strong belief in truth, they had no fear of man. This high degree of self-assurance enabled them to speak boldly, even when their words were not compliant to the power structures around them. It was these very qualities—intellectual prowess, fearless and contagious conviction of truth and magnetic temperament—that attracted people to their cause and, at the same time, eventually got them into trouble, a lot of trouble. They actively took their stand against evil and thus they became revolutionaries. The governing authorities arrested and executed them for seditious activity. Both died young, at approximately the same age, but they live on through their followers around the world.

Yet, there are two glaring differences between these two revolutionaries. Though both passionately fought for just causes, their methods were completely opposite. In fact, they were drastically contradictory. One approved of violent means to achieve his goals while the other trusted in a much different approach to bring about change.

The violence that the first revolutionary espoused caused him to become the dragon he went forth to slay. This fierce crusader killed and executed countless men in a cold-hearted, callous manner for his radical cause.

A small snippet from his diary, written during the beginning of the uprising he helped commandeer, reveals his chillingly logical belief in violence for the cause of his revolution. He shares his thoughts on the first man he executed:

> The situation was uncomfortable for the people and for Eutimio [the man who was to be executed] so I ended the problem giving him a shot with a .32 [calibre] pistol in the right side of the brain...He gasped a little while and was dead.[2]

History reveals to us that Eutimio Guerra was the first of many men executed by Che Guevara, the designated henchman to Fidel Castro's communist revolution. After Castro's rebel forces had won their revolution over the oppressive Cuban government, Guevara became the Chief Prosecutor in charge of the Comisión de Depuración (Cleansing Commission). He relished his role in overseeing a committee responsible to enact military justice and purify the country of enemies to the Cuban revolution. In the Fort La Cabaña, Havana, Che Guevara "took to his task with a singular determination, and the old walls of the fort rang out nightly with the fusillades of the firing squads."[3]

Guevara justified his essential role in overseeing these executions as an important task in assuring that his revolution succeeded in a letter to a friend: "The executions by firing squads are not only a necessity for the people of Cuba, but also an imposition by the people."[4]

The connection between violence and revolution remained with Che to the end. In 1967, while fighting for his communist revolution, Che Guevara was captured by Bolivian soldiers and executed. For years, his burial place was kept secret by the Bolivian government, in an effort to end the memory of his charismatic revolution. However, legends tend to grow in the guise of mysterious death and Che Guevara became a folk hero. His premature execution and the accompanying secrecy concerning his burial site vaulted him to the upper echelon of celebrated heroes. In 1997, his body was discovered and exhumed from Bolivia. Today his bones are enshrined in Cuba under a monument memorializing his life.

Che Guevara can no longer lead his revolution. In fact, it can be argued that his efforts failed miserably. The very thing he fought against has now taken over his legacy. Ironically, though Guevara despised capitalistic greed, his legend has become a money-making machine for rich entrepreneurs who have taken advantage of his legend. The famous graphic of his face is one of the world's most universally merchandized images. It is hawked everywhere and can be seen on all sorts of trinkets—key chains, posters, clocks, hats, T-shirts and even bikinis. Many people purchase these items without knowing anything about the man.

I will never forget watching a rich businessman drive past me in his Lexus, sipping an iced latte, while wearing a T-shirt with the face of Che Guevara emblazoned on the front. I could never picture this man as a subversive communist revolutionary for the poor. If only he understood what Che Guevara represented.

The disturbing irony of the Che Guevara mystique is that many of these tacky souvenir items are made in factories located in underdeveloped countries by people earning pennies for their labour. These oppressed factory workers are the very ones that Guevara fought to free from the tyranny of poverty imposed by corrupt governments and the rich upper class. The very thing he revolted against has overtaken his legacy.

Though Che Guevara left a record of violence and terror in his wake, the second revolutionary was the complete opposite. He, too, died for his cause, but he never embraced violent methods. Jesus Christ's revolution was based on spiritual weapons, as opposed to death and destruction. In comparing Che Guevara with Jesus Christ, it is clear that though their revolutions were just causes, their methodologies were polar opposite. Jesus used spiritual powers of peace in his rebellion while Che can be known as the godfather of terrorism.

Richard A. Horsely and Neil Asher Silberman describe Jesus' mission as a revolution in *The Message and the Kingdom*:

> In Jesus' preaching, the coming of the kingdom of God meant a revolution in the way people behaved toward each other and their recognition that they should have no Caesars, tetrarchs, or other overlords above them except for the one God and creator of the world. In practical terms, that meant rejecting the rule of all powers and returning to the pure covenantal system under which Israelites—and indeed all peoples—would be considered to be brothers and sisters under God. In modern political terms, that might be called a revolution…The kingdom of God was indeed at hand if they believed it—not a

dream, not a vision of heaven, not a spiritual state, but a social transformation here and now in the very fields they plowed and the very villages they lived in, if only they rejected injustice and heeded the commandments of God.[5]

In a day and age when oppressive powers ruled Jesus' world, his new kingdom message and active implementation of its new way of life meant certain conflict with the powerful rulers of his land. He was a dangerous revolutionary radical on a mission for peace and equality—a mission they did not support.

But the final glaring discrepancy between Che Guevara and Jesus Christ is this. Che Guevara lies in a tomb in Santa Clara, Cuba. His Cuban gravesite is recognized as a major historical site and a reminder that Guevara's revolution is over. However, the tomb of Jesus is empty. He is no longer there. His revolution is not over! He is still the commander and chief of his radical, subversive movement—his empty grave is proof.

The earth shattering reality is that Jesus is alive and his revolution continues.

NOTES

[1] *Chocolat.* Directed by Lasse Hallström. Toronto: Alliance Atlantis, 2000.

[2] Jon Lee Anderson, *Che Guevara: A Revolutionary Life* (New York: Grove Press, 1997), 237.

[3] Ibid., 386.

[4] Ibid., 375.

[5] Richard A. Horsely and Neil Asher Silberman, *The Message and the Kingdom* (Minneapolis: Augsburg Fortress, 1997), 54-56.

CHAPTER TWO

THE REVOLUTION CONTINUES

"There was a time when the church was very powerful. It was during that period when the early Christians rejoiced when they were deemed worthy to suffer for what they believed. In those days the church was not merely a thermometer that recorded the ideas and principles of popular opinion; it was a thermostat that transformed the mores of society. Whenever the early Christians entered a town the power structure got disturbed and immediately sought to convict them for being 'disturbers of the peace' and 'outside agitators.' But they went on with the conviction that they were 'a colony of heaven,' and had to obey God rather than man. They were small in number but big in commitment. They were too God-intoxicated to be 'astronomically intimidated.' They brought an end to such ancient evils as infanticide and gladiatorial contest."

Martin Luther King Jr.

Everything about Jesus points to a revolution.

For example, consider how his followers operated as a group. I find it interesting that even before the crucifixion of Jesus, his disciples often took on the characteristics of a revolutionary, clandestine movement. Yes, many times they appeared in public, performing kingdom works, but at other times they were not so public with their activity.

A good example of this is seen in how their last supper with Christ was secretive. They were like a rebel group, holding a covert underground meeting under the watchful eyes of the police, complete with a special signal and a secret saying to alert them to where the meeting was to take place:

> As you enter the city, a man carrying a jar of water will meet you. Follow him to the house he enters, and say to the owner of the house, "The Teacher asks: Where is the guest room, where I may eat the Passover with my disciples?" He will show you a large upper room, all furnished. Make preparations there." They left and found things just as Jesus had told them. (Lk 22:10-13)

The difficulty facing the authorities to crack this clandestine group was so great that they resorted to bribing an insider, Judas, for information. Why such secrecy? Simple. Revolution was in the air, and often, when revolutionary plans are being made, there is a need for secret meetings.

Jesus' revolutionary credentials are also evidenced in how he died. The Romans used crucifixion as a form of capital punishment for anyone who opposed them and who they deemed enemies of the state. This horrible method of torture was an effective, coercive instrument the Roman government used to intimidate any would-be revolutionary to submit to their authority. The fact that Jesus was crucified on this instrument of capital torture is proof alone that he was a recognizable revolutionary.

THE EARLY CHURCH: A REVOLUTIONARY MOVEMENT

The early followers of Jesus understood that their leader was a rebel. They recognized that his resurrection from the grave meant that the revolution was to be carried on. For them, the Easter experience of the cross and the resurrection of Jesus were essential. The cross had put an end to the old world order of sin and its resulting oppression and injustice; the resurrection signalled the beginning of a new world order—the entering of the kingdom of God. The empty tomb was a sign of victory. Jesus had conquered the enemy of evil—the devil and all forms of sin, such as the unjust power structures of the Roman Empire. The resurrection was the fuel that empowered the early church to go out and proclaim the manifestation of Jesus' all-encompassing reign. To the church, the death and resurrection of Jesus Christ are pivotal epochs in the history of civilization. They are signs that the kingdom of God, under the Lordship of Jesus Christ, is now come.

This is why the early church celebrated the Lord's Supper in feast-like fashion. Every time they broke the bread and drank the cup they celebrated the words of Jesus: "This is my body given to you…This cup is the **new covenant in my blood**, which is poured out for you" (Lk 22:19,20, emphasis added). Christ's death installed a new covenant, the kingdom reign of God, and his resurrection authorized the immense power of this kingdom that we are now part of. To the early believers, this was revolutionary music to their ears as they lived out the kingdom of God in the midst of the dying empire of the world.

They also paid the price of revolutionary martyrdom.

The apostles were also radicals, executed as revolutionaries by the ruling powers of their day. Some were crucified or put to the sword. Others were torn apart by animals, boiled alive or speared to death. Their deaths should not surprise us, as revolutionaries are often executed by the powers that be to squelch opposition. The deaths of the apostles demonstrate that they continued the Jesus revolution so effectively that they were killed for the cause. But the revolution continued in the lives of the early believers who came to know Christ through the ministry of the apostles.

JESUS' RADICAL WORDS OF REVOLUTION

The apostles had effectively passed on the radical words of Jesus, in obedience to their mandate:

> All authority in heaven and on earth has been given to me. Therefore go and make disciples of all nations, baptizing them in the name of the Father and of the Son and of the Holy Spirit, and teaching them to obey everything I have commanded you. And surely I am with you always, to the very end of the age. (Mt 28:18-20)

Most people overlook the revolutionary ramifications of Jesus' words here.

When Jesus said "All **authority** in heaven and on earth has been given to me," he laid claim over every physical and spiritual kingdom, king and person. By making such a statement, Jesus declared himself lord of all and polarized himself and his movement against any world or religious power that stood in opposition to his will. This is a true revolutionary statement if ever there was one. It is a loud declaration, proclaiming that Jesus trumps all things. His reign now has universal ramifications. Humanity has only two options: join the Jesus movement or stand in opposition of Christ. The early Christians understood this truth and, with the confidence of the resurrection of Christ fresh in their minds, were able to declare, even in the face of death, "Jesus is Lord!"

Jesus then includes his followers to join his revolution by commissioning his band of ragtag rebels to "go and make disciples of all nations." Jesus does not hold his authority solely for himself; he commissions his followers to challenge all people to give a 100 percent commitment to the cause of Christ through baptism, a true sign of ultimate submission. This seriousness of the act of baptism and its symbolic tie with the kingdom reign of Jesus holds great significance.

The truth behind this radical sacrament took on special meaning to me while I was studying in Bible college. I had become close friends with an African student who had come over from his country as a new Christian. One day we were talking about his life back in Africa and he told me that his father was a king of a tribe in his home country. As a son of the king my friend had a rosy future ahead of him with all sorts of wonderful benefits befitting royalty— money, honour and even many wives. He told me that on the day he became a Christian his family was disappointed in him. His father was a Muslim and wanted his son to pursue the Qur'an and he tried to persuade his son to recant his decision to follow Jesus. It didn't work. The harder he pressured his son to deny Jesus the stronger his son's faith in Christ became. Yet the father still loved his son very much, and the many wonderful privileges of being the son of the king were still available to my friend. However, everything changed the day my friend was baptized. When his father heard of his son's baptism he immediately disowned him from the family. The son was driven out of the village and all his royal rights were taken away. His family actually held a funeral ceremony declaring him dead.

There was my friend—all alone, living in Canada, with no family ties. All he had left was Jesus. But, according to my friend, Jesus is all he needed.

When my friend finished his story, I was stunned. How could a loving father do such a thing? As a father of two beautiful children, I could never imagine cutting them off from me, no matter what they did. I couldn't help but ask what changed his father's heart from being the warm loving dad that accepted his son as a Christian to the cold-hearted father that formally declared his son dead. My friend replied:

> The answer is easy. I was baptized. When I was baptized things changed forever. You see, everyone in my village knew Christians. They are no problem to my people. My tribe accepts them. But when a Christian gets real serious about Jesus he gets baptized, and things change. He is immediately viewed as being a radical. My people know that when one is baptized he turns his back on everything but Jesus. Baptized people are dangerous to the ways of our culture. They see things in a different light and live by a different set of rules, and this always leads to conflict.

A few weeks after our conversation, an announcement was made at our school asking us to report any strange looking people loitering around on campus. Word had leaked out that my friend had a bounty placed on his head by his father. Now he was living under a death threat.

This is the seriousness of his faith, and it demonstrates the significance of baptism.

The early church lived under similar conditions. Jesus commanded that his followers be baptized because they were joining a revolutionary movement that demanded a whole-hearted surrender to the cause of Christ. These early Christians understood that their allegiance was with the kingdom of God over and above the Roman Empire, and they lived accordingly. Baptism was a visible, public sign that showed that they were dead to the old world system, with Caesar as ruler, and made alive to a new world order, the kingdom of God, with Jesus as their supreme ruler. By declaring "Jesus is Lord," they renounced "Caesar is Lord" and paid the price for such insubordination.

These baptized radicals were to "obey everything I have commanded you." These commands of Jesus were not just something to learn about, they were to be lived out. Obedience was more than head knowledge—it implied action. Thus, the early Christians attempted to live out the actions of Christ as recorded in the Gospels.

Clearly, it was effective. Church historians report that before the reign of the emperor Constantine, Christians were persecuted for their uncompromising commitment to the movement that Jesus initiated.

With the instalment of the "kingdom of God" reign of Jesus there was now an inevitable kingdom conflict occurring between the Roman establishment and the Jesus movement. These baptized and trained Jesus followers were now thrust into an insurrectionary role against the societal norms of Roman culture. The early Christians faced opposition because their revolutionary actions flew in the face of Roman cultural norms.

These Christians were a different breed. They refused to participate in the slave trade. They took their stance against the cultic practices established by empire religion. They actively cared for the marginalized in their society, abandoned by the Roman government as a parasitic drain on their populace. In a divided society, torn apart by classism, sexism and racism, the early Christians modelled the kingdom of God by treating everyone as equal and sharing with one another whenever one was in need. So great was their love for each other that outsiders derisively labelled them as the third race.[1] The first race was the Romans, who perceived themselves as the superior civilization. The second race was the Jews, whose strong cultural and religious customs isolated them from other nationalities. The third race, then, was this strange group of Christians who openly embraced both Jew and Gentile, rich and poor, male and female, accepting one another as brothers and sisters in Christ Jesus. They were thought unpatriotic to Rome because they refused military service and refused to bow down to the emperor. They recognized Christ as their leader, and their revolutionary actions were part and parcel of their declaration of allegiance to Christ's kingdom.

Their subversive actions cost them dearly. Many lost jobs; others were severely mistreated and disowned by their families, while many more were martyred by the Roman emperor. Yet, even in the midst of great persecution, the Jesus movement grew by leaps and bounds. Tertullian wrote: "The blood of the martyrs is the seed of the church."

THE END OF THE REVOLUTION?

However, all of this changed with the emperor Constantine, who legalized Christianity and made it into an acceptable religion. One of the stories behind Constantine's change of heart is based on a miraculous victory that his forces had over an enemy with a vast advantage over his Roman legion. In jubilation of his miraculous victory, Constantine inquired about a strange vision he had of a cross at the beginning of the battle. He asked his military advisors if they knew what this symbol meant and was informed that the cross was the sign of the Christian god. He attributed his military victory to this Christian god, and to honour him, Constantine legalized Christianity.[2] He zealously baptized his armies into the church, put the sign of the cross on military weapons and handed over the pagan temples and priests to the Christians.

It was Constantine's acceptance of Christianity as a state religion that drained much of the revolutionary energy out of the Jesus movement. The legalization of Christianity gave the church power, and the once-radical movement transformed from a revolution into a religion. Christendom was birthed, and true Christianity was profoundly negatively impacted by its new partnership with political power.[3]

Seemingly overnight, the early church traded in its radical subversive movement for a state religion, with temples, priests and rituals. The bold message about the coming of the kingdom of God was compromised for acceptance by the kingdom of the world. Just like Satan's temptation of Christ in the desert, the church was offered "the kingdoms of the world and their splendour" (Mt 4:8). Jesus never fell for Satan's tricks, but the church wasn't as wise.

They fell hook, line and sinker for the temptation of power. Little did the early church know how their partnership with Constantine would weaken their prophetic voice and hinder their radical movement of the bringing in of the kingdom of God.

WARNINGS FROM A REVOLUTIONARY

In the Book of Revelation, John, the exiled revolutionary, writes to the persecuted church to encourage them not to compromise in following Jesus. As a prisoner guilty of treason, John had to use codes to get his message across to his readers so that the Roman guards who monitored his letters would allow them to pass through the strict criteria they used to filter out any material that they deemed anti-establishment. So in his letter, John used many descriptive images to point out the evils of Rome, without being too obvious.

Unfortunately, too many preachers today tend to forget this. Instead of using the Book of Revelation as a reliable tool in examining our present-day issues of political injustice, economic inequality, consumerist greed, increased militarism and environmental disasters, these "prophetic" preachers use them to point to future events. By focusing only on the "end times" they avoid dealing with the contemporary issues that the Book of Revelation addresses.

The context of John's revelation is extreme persecution. He shares how the kingdom of God and the kingdom of this world are in deep conflict with one another. John describes the kingdom of the world (in the context of the Roman Empire) as being under satanic influences. The kingdom of the world is referred to as Babylon, one of the most evil empires in the history of the Old Testament, which he describes as being a great whore who sacrifices people and births great injustices in order to feed her rich appetite for material comforts and gain.

When you understand the context of John's writing, you cannot help but realize that what he is saying about Babylon authoritatively applies to our present-day situation. Babylon, the kingdom of the world, is still active in producing enormous bloodshed for monetary gain and temporal luxuries. This great whore seduces us with her surgically enhanced body while whispering to us with her collagen lips how wonderful we will feel if we only lay down in her arms and commit to her ways. Our capitalistic religion worships her by preaching the importance of money and possessions as things to be pursued, as ultimate priority, which is contrary to the teachings of Jesus, who told us that to love God and to love people must be our main concern (Lk 10:27). Babylon is destroying people's lives and decimating our environment. And many people get into bed with this great whore.

THE RISE OF CHRISTENDOM, THE DEMISE OF JESUS' REVOLUTION

John warned against the intoxicating powers of the great whore. Yet, the early church was still enticed to join the empire under the rule of Constantine. The pagan priests, who once led people in the worship of idols, were now commissioned by Constantine to be Christian priests, and they transformed their pagan temples into places of Christian worship. These priests also changed their pagan rituals into Christian rites. They blessed the armies of Rome and supported the policies of the emperor. And the radical subversive power of the Jesus revolution was quickly immobilized.

Priestly hierarchies came into being, and soon they incorporated Greco-

Roman philosophy and ritual into the Jesus movement. Dependence on Jesus and the power of the Holy Spirit were replaced by blind trust in religious leaders, rituals and temples.

At one time, the Christians openly declared that they didn't need Rome's priests, temples and rituals. For these early radicals, Jesus was their high priest and the only priest they needed. Their temples were located any place they gathered and their rituals were simple—prayer, reading of the word, baptism and the Lord's Supper. But now the radical foundation of a movement based on declaring "Jesus is Lord" slowly crumbled into a state of co-dependency on the various competing lords of a growing religious establishment with paid priests, elaborate rites and ornate temples.

Though this happened centuries ago, the influence of Christendom lives on today, as Babylon continues to influence the church. Like the early Christians that embraced compromise with Rome, many of us have also chosen to endorse the empire of health and wealth, commercialism and consumerism. The religion of Babylonian Christianity is proven alive and well when presidents and dictators, armies and corporations, Hollywood and media moguls are blessed and endorsed by Christians who have sacrificed their prophetic voice for power and influence. Today we also have ornate temples where specialized religious rituals take place that can only be performed by ordained professional priests and ministers. What happened to the Jesus revolution?

In light of how far we have diverged from the revolutionary movement Jesus initiated, one can argue that, like Che Guevara's legacy, the legacy of Jesus was a failure. There have been crusades, wars and torture conducted in the name of Christ. People still hate in the name of Jesus. Christian religion and division are still strong. The very thing that Jesus despised has been done in his name. The influence of Constantine lives on!

IT IS TIME FOR A JESUS REVOLUTION

But one must keep in mind the fact that most legacies apply to dead people. Jesus is alive! The grave is still empty! Jesus is still on the throne and active in building his revolution. Thank God that Jesus is still at work. His uprising still beckons and he wants you to join his movement. It is time for a renewed revolution of people who are willing to stand up and shout out to a world that despises the things of God that Jesus is Lord! It is time once again for a Jesus revolution.

NOTES

[1] David J. Bosch, *Transforming Mission* (Maryknoll: Orbis Books, 2007), 48.

[2] There are other theories for why Constantine legalized Christianity. One is that he was desperately seeking a way to unite his divided empire to divert political destruction. This theory claims that Constantine made up his vision as a way to unite his empire under one common world religion. This would fit in well with John's revelation from the Book of Revelation.

[3] Alan Hirsch, *The Forgotten Ways: Reactivating the Missional Church* (Grand Rapids: Brazos Press, 2007), 60, quotes Rodney Stark: "Far too long, historians have accepted the claim that the conversion of the Emperor Constantine (ca. 285-337) caused the triumph of Christianity. To the contrary, he destroyed its most attractive and dynamic aspects, turning a high-intensity, grassroots movement into an arrogant institution controlled by an elite."

CHAPTER THREE

JESUS' REVOLUTIONARY DECLARATION OF INDEPENDENCE

"Revolutions are not to be evaluated in terms of the terror they spread, nor of the destruction they cause, but rather in terms of the alternatives they are able to offer. In its missionary outreach into the Greco-Roman world, the early church offered such alternatives."

David J. Bosch[1]

Each year, on the fourth of July, Americans celebrate their birthday as a nation with community barbecues, flag waving and fireworks. The basis for these festivities is a document written in 1776, the Declaration of Independence, that boldly declares the will of the American colonies to be free from British rule. This historic manuscript became the foundation for the American Revolution and illustrates the fact that every revolution must start with a clear declaration of self-determination away from the ruling powers that be. These radical documents are very important in building a strong framework in which a revolution can withstand the pressures that will inevitably resist it. Without such a declaration, a revolution can never grow into a powerful, transforming movement. Thus, it is of vital importance that Jesus' revolutionary movement have its own declaration of independence and, as we shall soon discover, Jesus himself made such a statement.

In Luke 4:18-19, we come across Jesus' declaration of independence. These verses, based upon Old Testament prophecy, clearly constitute his revolutionary intent in which we, as followers of Jesus, can draw some important principles to guide our movement. However, before we examine Jesus' revolutionary announcement it is important that we take a few steps back in time and understand everything that had happened up to this point in the life of Christ.

Before his return to Nazareth, Jesus was making quite the name for himself. It was an exciting time for Jesus, and his popularity was on the rise. He had already gained a reputation as a brilliant teacher and successful miracle worker. The renowned John the Baptist had publically honoured Jesus as one who "is more powerful than I, the thongs of whose sandals I am not worthy to stoop down and untie" (Mk 1:7). John went on to say, "I baptize you with water, but he [Jesus] will baptize you with the Holy Spirit" (Mk 1:8). These words of endorsement, from such an enigmatic figure as John the Baptist, would have caused a stir among the many people who followed John, resulting in group anticipation and curiosity about Jesus. In this sense, John the Baptist was very successful in drawing attention to Jesus and his fledgling ministry.

Jesus was gaining popularity among the general public. People were attracted to his strong teaching ministry and accompanying miracles. At this point, Jesus had already changed the water to wine at the wedding in Cana (Jn 2:11), challenged the woman at the well concerning her private life through miraculous insight (she in turn told everyone in her town about this wonderful man named Jesus, which led to more people becoming followers of Christ, Jn 4:28ff) and was involved in the healing of a high-ranking official's son (Jn 4:46-54).[2] All of these recorded acts of Jesus (and others unrecorded, Jn 21:25) helped to increase his popularity. Luke writes, "Jesus returned to Galilee in the power of the Spirit, and news about him spread through the whole countryside. He taught in their synagogues and everyone praised him" (4:14-15).

Jesus now returned home as the guest speaker in the synagogue in Nazareth, where he grew up (Lk 4:16). Likely, this place of worship was jam-packed to hear Jesus speak. The mood in the synagogue that day would have been electric as the large crowd slowly filled the synagogue to hear Jesus. Hometown pride would have been on display to welcome one of their own who was now famous. It was here, in the midst of this festive atmosphere, that Jesus chose to reveal his declaration of independence by intentionally opening to a specific passage taken from the scroll of Isaiah. Luke recounts:

> The scroll of the prophet Isaiah was handed to him. Unrolling it, he found the place where it is written: "The Spirit of the Lord is upon me, because he has anointed me to preach good news to the poor. He has sent me to proclaim freedom for the prisoners and recovery of sight for the blind, to release the oppressed, to proclaim the year of the Lord's favour." Then he rolled up the scroll, gave it back to the attendant and sat down. The eyes of everyone in the synagogue were fastened on him, and he began by saying to them, "Today this Scripture is fulfilled in your hearing." (4:17–21)

Note the reaction of his listeners: every eye in the synagogue was staring right at him. The people were awestruck with Jesus. This is because Jesus deliberately chose to read the "Jubilee" prophecy from Isaiah 61, knowing, like any good Jew of his day, that this was a well-known prophetic passage pointing to the coming messiah. It gave the Jewish people hope that one day their redeemer would come to Israel and destroy all of her oppressors, resulting in the restoration of a new kingdom reign. Jesus' listeners, who suffered under the cruel reign of their Roman conquerors, no doubt wondered if he was this promised messiah. To this Jesus answered with an incredible affirmative saying: "Today this Scripture is fulfilled in your hearing."

By reading from this passage of Isaiah, Jesus hits the jackpot of clarity in describing the driving purpose of his mission. This was his revolutionary declaration of independence. There was now a new reign on earth, the kingdom of God had begun. Jesus could not have made it clearer: he is the promised messiah, the king who will establish his rule and introduce the year of the Lord's favour or, in biblical terms, the "Year of Jubilee."

WHAT IS JUBILEE?

A passage in Leviticus regarding Jubilee provides understanding to the statement made by Jesus:

> Count off seven sabbaths of years—seven times seven years— so that the seven sabbaths of years amount to a period of forty-nine years. Then have the trumpet sounded everywhere on the tenth day of the seventh month; on the Day of Atonement sound the trumpet throughout your land.

Consecrate the fiftieth year and proclaim liberty throughout the land to all its inhabitants. It shall be a jubilee for you; each one of you is to return to his family property and each to his own clan. The fiftieth year shall be a jubilee for you; do not sow and do not reap what grows of itself or harvest the untended vines...If one of your countrymen becomes poor and sells some of his property...if he does not acquire the means to repay him [the buyer], what he sold will remain in the possession of the buyer until the Year of Jubilee. It will be returned in the Jubilee, and he can then go back to his property...If one of your countrymen becomes poor among you and sells himself to you, do not make him work as a slave. He is to be treated as a hired worker or a temporary resident among you; he is to work for you until the Year of Jubilee. Then he and his children are to be released, and he will go back to his own clan and to the property of his forefathers. (25:8–11, 25, 28, 39–41)

The Year of Jubilee was to occur every 50 years as a safeguard against human greed and exploitation. God knew that the heart of man is very deceitful (Jer 17:9), especially when it comes to materialistic gain, so he came up with a sagacious law guaranteeing that there would never be a huge income gap between the rich and the poor. God's Jubilee brought many practical solutions to deal with potential oppression in the nation of Israel.

The advantages of this institution were manifold. It would prevent the accumulation of land on the part of a few to the detriment of the community at large. It would render it impossible for anyone to be born to absolute poverty, since everyone had hereditary land. It would preclude inequalities produced by extremes of riches and poverty. It would eliminate slavery. It would afford a fresh opportunity to those who were reduced by adverse circumstances to begin again their career of industry in the patrimony that they had temporarily forfeited. It would periodically rectify the disorders that crept into the state in the course of time, preclude the division of the people into nobles and plebeians and preserve the theocracy inviolate.[3]

Jubilee was great news for the poor. On this momentous occasion, the rich were to give back the land they bought from the poor. Children sold into slavery were to be set free. All debts were to be forgiven, resulting in the freeing of captives from debtors prison. Jubilee was to guarantee that every person in Israel was to be free to control his or her own assets to succeed in a fair market. What an amazing economic plan from God.

THE SIGNIFICANCE OF JUBILEE FOR JESUS' LISTENERS

Jubilee held great significance for Jesus' listeners, who suffered greatly under the oppression of Rome. The conquering Romans, through Caesar Augustus, had declared Pax Romana, which was a devious way of saying "total peace within the Roman Empire." However, this "Roman peace" was enforced through severe political violence against the occupied countries. Pax Romana was so violent that the historian Tacitus wrote:

> [We] have sought in vain to escape [the Romans'] oppression by obedience and submissiveness. [They are] the plunderers of the world…If the enemy is rich, they are rapacious, if poor, they lust for dominion. Not East, not West has satiated them…They rob, butcher, plunder, and call it "empire"; and where they make a desolation, they call it peace.[4]

In Palestine, political relationships were established between the Roman army and the aristocracy of Israel. The rich held positions of power as long as they worked for Rome's interests. The hereditary priestly class and elders, who represented the richest families of Jerusalem, ruled the Sanhedrin and were in cahoots with Rome. W. Philip Keller writes,

> The atrocious wrongs and devilish deeds done in the temple defy our imagination. It is hard to realize that some 20 thousand priests and helpers in and around Jerusalem survived like parasites draining the life blood and hard-earned savings from the people who came there to worship. It has been estimated that the average annual income derived from the temple trade exceeded 35 million dollars. In this the hierarchy of priests and scholars lived in pompous, pious ease and luxury. Some were so skilled at manipulating money that they had become inordinately wealthy. Their hearts' affection was supposed to be in heaven, but they made very sure their sensual souls were glutted with silver on earth…They banqueted in abundance,

wrapped in their rich gowns of gold brocade, while hungry beggars and poor peasants lay prostrate in their rags on the temple steps.[5]

The religious leaders' response to Roman domination was two-fold. The Sadducees were silent to injustice and friendly with the Roman Empire, generally prospering off Roman oppression by lining their pockets with empirical money. On the opposite scale were the Pharisees, religious fundamentalists who responded to Roman injustice by casting further judgement on the Jewish people. These religious legalists had no mercy toward the poor, the sick and the prostitutes, as they saw their suffering as the result of unholy living. These Pharisees believed that the solution to Roman occupation was to establish a theocracy by enacting religious laws that, if obeyed, would usher in the messiah, who would conquer Israel's enemies. Unfortunately, the Pharisees viewed the poor, sick and sexually immoral as guilty ones who by their sinful behaviour were delaying God's divine rule. Theologically speaking, the Sadducees and Pharisees were on completely opposite sides of the spectrum, but even in their differences they were part of the oppressive system that dominated Palestine. Thus, Jesus opposed them.

One of the greatest burdens placed on the backs of the people was heavy taxation in the form of religious tithes and the temple tax. Every Jew was expected to set aside a significant portion of his produce in the form of a priestly tithe, as well as other forms of sacred donations, including the annual payment of a temple tax. These forms of religious duty were an unbearable load for a poor and conquered people to carry and contributed greatly to the poverty that was rampant in the land.

Making matters worse, the conquering Romans took full advantage of their power, extracting anything they deemed necessary from the subjugated populace they controlled. People were forced to give up their possessions, food, land and even their time in forced labour to benefit the conquering army!

Greed, oppression and high taxes created rampant poverty among the majority of Palestine. Most of the populace of Israel were forced to sell land and home to fulfill the tax demands. Since the aristocracy, backed by the Romans, were the only ones that had money to purchase land from the poor Jews, the cycle of greed and oppression deepened. The rich got richer and more powerful and the poor got poorer and more vulnerable. Those who could not find jobs became slaves, and many others were forced to go to prison because of their inability to pay debts.

This is why Pax Romana produced uprisings against the oppressors, leading to more violence. In response to these insurrections, the Romans invented crucifixion to intimidate any potential insurrectionist. To enforce a psychological advantage, the Roman military would often stage crucifixions in major thoroughfares, leaving the suffering criminal on the cross to die a slow and agonizing death. The screams of agony from the dying man were constant warnings to the people not to rebel against the state.

Jesus: Hope for the Oppressed

Jesus was born as a poor Jewish peasant into this environment of extreme injustice. God was now on the side of the poor. His declaration of independence was great news for the poor and the oppressed and extremely bad news for those who were rich from unjust means. As Jesus said:

> The Spirit of the Lord is upon me, because he has anointed me
> to preach good news to the poor. He has sent me to proclaim
> freedom for the prisoners and recovery of sight for the blind,
> to release the oppressed, to proclaim the year of the Lord's
> favour. (Lk 4:18-19)

By declaring Jubilee as his mission, Jesus was siding with all the rejects of society—the poor who were prisoners in debtors prison, blind beggars and those who were oppressed by the system that favoured the rich over the poor. Jubilee was about helping the poor. Jesus is for the poor. The poor are his priority, his passion and his heartbeat.

Now imagine what it would be like on that first day of Jubilee. Could you imagine the joy the poor received? They were released from prison, restored to their families and got their fields and houses back. But the rich had to forgive all debt, give back the land they had bought and release their cheap labour. This is probably why there is no record of the Jews obeying this commandment. Jewish history never once records that the year of "Jubilee" was acted upon.

The Significance of Jubilee Today

Jesus was declaring "I will act out Jubilee! My salvation is Jubilee! My mission is Jubilee!" He still is saying "It is the year of Jubilee!" Philip Yancey aptly describes how we North Americans miss out on the meaning of Jesus' Jubilee mission:

From the comfort of a middle-class church in a wealthy country like the US, I easily lose sight of the radical core of Jesus' message. To help correct my vision, I have read sermons that come out of the Christian-based communities in the Third World. The gospel through Third World eyes looks very different from the gospel as preached in many US churches. The poor and the unlearned cannot always identify Jesus' mission statement as a quotation from Isaiah, but they hear it as good news indeed. They understand the great reversal, not as an abstraction but as God's promise of defiant hope and Jesus' challenge to his followers. Regardless of how the world treats me, the poor and the sick have assurance, because of Jesus, that God knows no undesirables.[6]

ACTING OUT JUBILEE IN OUR CHURCHES TODAY

Often when preaching on Jubilee, I tantalize my listeners by telling them that if we obeyed the Jubilee law we would never be in debt for more than 50 years. Imagine what would happen if we lived by this "Jubilee" law? No more credit card or college tuition debt. No more car or mortgage payments. Yet, if we like Jubilee because it benefits us personally, we would need to take it further, to act out Jubilee as our mission to others wherever we go.

Imagine how Jubilee would give life back to our churches. We would have a reason and purpose behind our worship. Church would not just be a worship service where people seek God to bless them and meet their own needs. Instead, church would be as intended—a living organism, the body of Christ, in which Jesus, as the head, works through his people to enact his kingdom of justice everywhere we go. In other words, the church would be a movement of revolutionary Christians filled with the Spirit of Christ who live out the gospel truths in a dark and unjust world.

Imagine the impact the church will have if it stands on the side of the poor and oppressed? Locally, it would be involved with inner-city issues by providing education and job opportunities for those living in these communities. It would combat racism, sexism and all other forms of oppression that often birth poverty. Nationally, it would be involved in bringing justice to our countries of origin. As a Canadian, this means that we must work with our First Nations people in their fight for justice. Imagine what Jubilee means for them? Maybe it is time for us to revisit the many broken treaties we have unjustly participated in regarding the land and our indigenous peoples who were the first ones to inhabit our country. Jubilee would demand that we make things right with our First Nations brothers and sisters.

On a global scale, Jubilee becomes even more radical. It means the church must get involved in eliminating crippling developing world debt. Jubilee would demand that we figure out just ways to put an end to sweatshops and unfair trade practices. The church would also stand up for peace against unmerited warfare that results from our consumerist desire for self-protection. We would rally around the need to care for our environment, no matter the sacrificial cost to our standard of living.

Jubilee makes us take responsibility to understand what is happening in our world locally, nationally and globally so that we can work with Jesus in following his kingdom agenda. Jubilee demands that we get involved in our world both personally and politically. As Jubilee people, we understand that dictators, famines and wars are often the fruit of unjust practices that would never be tolerated if we practiced Jubilee. Most, if not all, poor countries were once vassals of colonizing nations or are now under political pressure exerted on them from new, more sophisticated colonizers who take advantage of poorer countries. Too often, underdeveloped nations are viewed as having value only because of what we can get from them. The people that live there and the conditions that they live in do not matter as long as we can get things we want from them as cheaply as possible. Jubilee would never allow this to happen.

GOD'S PREFERENTIAL TREATMENT OF THE POOR

Now, you might be thinking "Surely you are not saying that we must choose the poor for special ministry over and above everyone else?" No, I am not saying this—God is! In James we read "Has not God chosen those who are poor in the eyes of the world to be rich in faith and to inherit the kingdom he promised those who loved him?" (2:5).

God has a special love for the poor. In fact, the Bible refers to the poor over 2000 times! It is clearly evident that if we are to be followers of Jesus, the yardstick to measure our success is how we treat the poor.

The poor are the first, though not the only ones, on which God's attention focuses, and therefore, the church has no choice but to demonstrate solidarity with the poor. The poor have an epistemological privilege…There can be no doubt that both the Old Testament and in the ministry of Jesus there was a significant focus on the poor and their plight. The entire Bible, beginning with the story of Cain and Abel, mirrors God's predilection for the weak and abused of human history. Much of this ethos was preserved during the first centuries of the Christian church. After Constantine, and as the church got richer and more privileged, the poor were increasingly neglected or treated condescendingly. Yet even then powerful voices, in particularly from the circles of the monastic movement, continued to stress the Christian's inescapable responsibility in this regard…In a sense, then, the rediscovery of the poor in our own time is also a reaffirmation of an ancient theological tradition.[7]

Ministry to the poor is a priority of God.

Jesus' actions confirm this. Most of his ministry was to the poor. In the Gospels, Jesus calls low-class fishermen to follow him. He bestows value on prostitutes—women who had exhausted what little means of survival they had in a male-dominated society, who were left to sell their bodies to make enough money to live another day. He heals lepers, labelled unclean by their society and unable to hold down jobs due to their condition, and the lame, left as beggars. Jesus tells the rich young ruler to sell everything he has and give the money to the poor. Even the birth of Jesus was marked by a love for the poor and oppressed, as seen in Mary's great prayer in Luke 4:46-55: "He has brought down rulers from their thrones but has lifted up the humble. He has filled the hungry with good things but has sent the rich away empty." And who are the first people to hear the great birth announcement of Jesus in Bethlehem? Shepherds—the poorest of the poor in Jesus' day. It is clear that Jesus is all about the poor.

Yes, Jubilee is what Christ is all about and therefore must be what we are all about. Our Jubilee God forces us to ask this question: "Am I a Jubilee person? Am I passionate about serving the poor?"

True followers of Jesus take the plight of the poor seriously simply because

Jesus did. We believe that we are to fulfill Jesus' prayer: "As you sent me into the world, I have sent them into the world" (Jn 17:8). In other words, we are on the same mission as Jesus—a mission to the poor.

When I think of Jubilee, I cannot help but wonder what its implications are for the city I live in. Like any city in North America, my city has a fairly large population base living in poverty. Most of the poor are children from single parent homes led by mothers. These families live in government housing communities that sorely lack resources needed to make a neighbourhood safe and productive. Jobs are scarce, racism rampant and hopelessness seems to dominate the landscape.

Drug dealing and other criminal activities often appear viable options when you are poor and frequently present a daily temptation to make a fast buck. What follows is heartbreaking. In one of the communities we serve, a young man was shot in front of some children who were walking home from school one day. Yellow tape was set up to surround the crime scene and the police went door to door asking questions, but the children seemed unaffected. They just kept on playing in the front lawns of their apartment, like nothing had happened. Violence, guns and despondency are far too common in our inner-city communities, and when acts of violence occur, our children take no notice. Children should not have to live in dangerous neighbourhoods, where an errant bullet might find its way into their innocent bodies.

I know of a young 16-year-old girl who has been impacted by five shootings during her short lifespan. Her first experience with gun violence occurred when she was a child. Her friend was shot in the leg by a wayward bullet when they were playing together in at a community park. They were both 8 years old at the time of this shooting! The second shooting she encountered involved a 2-year-old baby girl from her neighbourhood who was shot and killed when a gang tried to execute her father. The little baby was shot in the head, and her father crippled by a hail of bullets in a drive by while he was putting his daughter in a child safety seat in the back of his car. The third incident of violence she experienced occurred when she was 10 years old. She saw a man with a handgun being chased by the police. They ran right by her as she stood frozen in the same playground where her friend had been shot only 2 years earlier. Then, when she was 15 years old, her friend was shot and killed. When she was 16 years old, another friend she knew was shot and stabbed to death.

While many of us have declared these inner-city communities as hopeless cases, Jesus doesn't; he hasn't given up on them. In fact, he looks at these communities and declares Jubilee over them and then he invites us to join him in bringing his Jubilee into these communities.

THE JUBILEE GOSPEL

My old response to such communities was that they needed to hear that they were sinners and they needed to be saved from their sins through Jesus Christ. It didn't matter that kids went to bed hungry at night or that 75 percent of the youth in the community dropped out of school. I thought that the gospel was about verbal witness and all we had to do is go and tell these people to get right with God. Now don't get me wrong, I believe that words are an important part of the gospel, but I now realize that words are only one element of the gospel. Jesus said he would bring freedom, recovery and release! The gospel is more than just words.

I work for an inner-city ministry called UrbanPromise Toronto that is concerned about the souls of those we serve. We want to see them come to the saving knowledge of Jesus Christ. But it doesn't end there. We also want them to experience the saving power of Jesus Christ to transform their circumstances! Consequently, our gospel is not just words, it is also actions. We don't just teach the Bible—we experience biblical truths with those in our communities. To us, Jubilee means becoming a daily presence in the neighbourhoods we are involved with. We befriend those in the community and genuinely care for each other. This creates a true family of God, as we share our lives with one another. And this is what Jesus did during his Jubilee mission—he dwelt among us!

> The Word was God…
> The Word became flesh and blood,
>   and moved into the neighbourhood.
> We saw the glory with our own eyes,
>   the one-of-a-kind glory,
>   like Father, like Son,
> Generous inside and out,
>   true from start to finish. (Jn 1:1-2, 14, *The Message*)

Too many of us have a limited gospel. We think that if we preach words and go to church every week we are doing our jobs. That is not Jubilee. Some of us feel so guilty because we have a hard time telling people the gospel. Well, I've got good news for you.

The gospel is not just telling someone they are a sinner and need Jesus; it is much more. The gospel is reading a book to a poor child, tutoring a kid who is struggling in school, chilling with teens in government housing, mentoring a teen in trouble with the law. The gospel is being the loving presence of God to the poor, oppressed and lonely. We can all do that. In this way our gospel is not just words but power! As St. Francis said, "Preach the gospel at all times and, if necessary, use words."

Loving actions empower the gospel to be experienced first. This leads to opportunities for you to share, with words, why you live as a Jubilee person. It gives you a foundation of authority, substance and influence upon which to preach about Jesus' saving power. It gives you the right to be heard.

I want to end this chapter by revisiting Luke 4:20: "The eyes of everyone in the synagogue were fastened on him." This audience reaction was the result of the fact that for years they anticipated the coming of messiah, who was to be anointed by God to bring the kingdom of God to earth. The Hebrew word for messiah means anointed one. Here was Jesus, in his hometown synagogue, reading from Isaiah 61, telling the people that he is the anointed one. He was proclaiming that he is the long-awaited messiah, who will bring the kingdom of God to earth! And what does this kingdom of God look like? Jubilee!

Now here is exciting news. The same Spirit that anointed Jesus is also upon you. If you are a Christian you can declare:

> The Spirit of the Lord is upon **me**, because he has anointed **me**
> to preach good news to the poor. He has sent **me** to proclaim
> freedom for the prisoners and recovery of sight for the blind,
> to release the oppressed, to proclaim the year of the Lord's
> favour. (Lk 4:18-19, emphasis added)

We, like Jesus, have the gifts and abilities, through the Spirit of God living in us, to serve the poor. We are specifically empowered and anointed to serve the poor, release the prisoner, free the oppressed and preach the good news. We are created and empowered to bring about Jubilee! And the eyes of everyone in our world are fastened upon us to see if we will act Jubilee. So how about it?

NOTES

[1] David J. Bosch, *Transforming Mission: Paradigm Shifts in Theology of Mission* (Maryknoll: Orbis Books, 1991), 47-48.

[2] I owe much to Orville E. Daniel's *A Harmony Of The Four Gospels: The New International Version* (Grand Rapids: Baker Books, 1996) in researching the activities of Christ.

[3] "Jubilee," *Easton's Bible Dictionary.*

[4] Obery M. Hendricks Jr., *The Politics Of Jesus* (New York: Doubleday Press, 2006), 51.

[5] W. Philip Keller, *Rabboni* (Grand Rapids: Fleming H. Revell, 1977), 91.

[6] Philip Yancey, *The Jesus I Never Knew* (Grand Rapids: Zondervan Publishing Co., 1995), 157.

[7] Bosch, 436.

CHAPTER FOUR

JESUS THE REVOLUTIONARY

I remember speaking at a church one Sunday on the topic of Jesus the Revolutionary. As I walked into the church auditorium, I couldn't help but notice a huge painting of Jesus that I found very disturbing. Framed in canvas was a Jesus that I could only describe as effeminate. His eyes were lifeless, his complexion milky white and his cheeks hollow. His beard was spotless and it encompassed his rosy red lips, which appeared to be filled in with red lipstick. Around his head was a bright yellow halo that created a dim glow upon his long, shiny, flowing hair. His appearance made him look like he had just stepped out of an expensive beauty salon. Needless to say, I could not help but refer to this picture of Jesus throughout my message as a central illustration of how we have done a great injustice to Jesus by attempting to neuter his radical personality. I wonder if I will ever be asked to preach there again.

The venerated Irish playwright George Bernard Shaw has been attributed to saying "In the beginning, God created man in his own image and man returned the favour by creating God into his own image."

I wonder if this is what we have done to Jesus. Perhaps the radical and revolutionary Jesus frightens us so much that we have tried to tame him into someone who is our divine cheerleader, someone who meaninglessly approves of our comfortable lifestyles. This hedonistic idol that we have created and now call Jesus is much easier to worship than the real Jesus who calls us to deny ourselves, take up our cross and follow him on a daily basis (Lk 9:23). We would much rather deal with our own personal and powerless happy Jesus than the one in the Gospels who told the rich young ruler to sell everything he has and give it to the poor (Mk 10:21).

TOTEMISM

In every culture of the world, from the highest forms of society to the lowest, it is evident that deep inside the heart of every man and woman is a soul. This deep spirituality, innate to all of us, drives humanity to worship someone greater than itself. Unfortunately, our human nature tends to satisfy this soul hunger for God by creating a god in our own image. Sociologists refer to this as "totemism"; we create our gods to embrace all the things we believe in. In doing this, we are able to control God and have him give us a divine stamp of approval to justify our own lifestyle choices.

A good example of totemism happened to me while on a trip to Washington D.C. I quickly became friends with an African American who worked at the hotel. Each morning, I headed to the hotel lobby for a bottle of orange juice, a newspaper and a visit with my new friend to discuss sports and other news of the day. We both shared a passion for basketball, and one morning, my friend invited me to join him and his buddies for a game of hoops at a local YMCA. I was free that evening, so I accepted. We met up after his shift, hopped into his car and went to his house to pick up his gear.

When we arrived at his house, I went in with him. We entered his living room, and he quickly bounded up the stairs into his room to grab his basketball gear. While I waited downstairs, I looked at the various pictures he had on his wall.

They were all standard household fare with the typical family portraits and various paintings of houses, trees and sunsets. However, in the midst of these domesticated bits and pieces, three distinctive pictures caught my eye. The first picture was of Malcolm X in his familiar black-framed glasses. The other, a depiction of Martin Luther King Jr. giving one of his famous speeches. And, in the middle, enshrined by these photographs of the great civil rights leaders of years past, was the famous painting of the Last Supper by Leonardo da Vinci.

However, the painting was markedly different than da Vinci's masterpiece. It had the same long table where Jesus was in his familiar spot in the middle of the twelve disciples. Yet, Jesus and his disciples were all black with afro-styled hair. As I was staring at the picture, my friend came down the stairs and asked me what I thought of his picture of Jesus and the disciples. I responded "I never knew Jesus was black." His response was classic: "Well, he was no honky either!"

My friend was right, Jesus certainly was no white honky, but he wasn't black either. We were both guilty of totemism. My Jesus was white, just like me and his Jesus was black, just like him. In fact, I have seen various pictures of Chinese Jesus, Indian Jesus, Russian Jesus, Native American Jesus and all other types of Jesus from various artist renditions all around the world.

We tend to make Jesus just like us so we can gain his favour. However, in doing this, we create God in our own image—a totem pole god that looks like us, speaks like us and thinks like us. This enables us to validate our value system and behaviour so that we can worship ourselves and, at the same time, try to satisfy our deep spiritual hunger.

HAVE WE CREATED OUR OWN JESUS?

Could it be that the church has created a Jesus that is gentle, meek and mild simply because the alternative scares us to death? Perhaps the weak, effeminate Jesus we see in religious paintings reveals more about ourselves than the real Jesus? Perhaps these portraits mirror the truth about our selfishness? *We, not Jesus,* are the soft ones who do not want to face the reality of the Lion of Judah who sits on the throne of heaven telling us what to do.

Maybe our propensity to constantly quote the polite scriptures about Jesus, instead of embracing the tough scriptures, reveals that we follow a deformed caricature of Jesus. Many of us have highlighted verses in our Bibles; how many of these verses are the real troubling, tough scriptures that demand of us a lifestyle of sacrifice and service? Or are they the nice, comforting verses that guarantee us divine blessings and favour?

The false teachers of the prosperity gospel have exploited our desire for a safe God, greatly profiting by selling products guaranteeing financial riches. They play on greediness and exploit the genuine needs of their followers with false promises. They never preach the truth about the homeless Jesus who had no place to lay his head. After all, in our consumerist society, who would ever want to follow a homeless man?

THE TRUTH ABOUT JESUS

The real Jesus is scary. A friend of mine once told me that when he became a Christian, Jesus ruined his safe little life! The real Jesus challenges us to change, to die to ourselves and to suffer for righteousness sake, especially on behalf of the poor and the outcast.

I remember a man gave me advice about putting my children to sleep. He said that the worst thing a parent could do was to read their children bedside stories about Jesus. In his opinion, stories of Jesus would guarantee that any child who heard them would have horrible nightmares. His advice makes sense, doesn't it?

Imagine reading to your child the stories about Jesus exorcising demons and then ending the story by giving your little son a soft kiss, saying a prayer and then turning off his light! Envisage telling your sweet little daughter how Jesus entered a church one day, whip in hand, and thrashed people and then ending the story by asking your daughter to say a prayer to Jesus before she goes to sleep. Or what if you read the story where Jesus said, "If anyone comes to me and does not hate his father and mother, his wife and children, his brothers and sisters—yes, even his own life—he cannot be my disciple" (Lk 14:26)?

Why is it that we don't underline these verses in our Bibles? The answer is simple. They make us too uncomfortable. We can't handle the truth about Jesus, so we deform his image to be safe. The real Jesus scares us, shakes us to the core. He challenges our self-reliance and comfortable lifestyle. He turns the little world that we have made safe for ourselves upside down, so we attempt to sterilize him by ignoring the tough revolutionary verses about Jesus and settle for a sanitized version.

BARTOLOMÉ ESTEBAN MURILLO

Michael Frost, an Australian evangelist and missiologist, shares a wonderful story about the great Spanish painter Bartolomé Esteban Murillo to illustrate the real Jesus.[1] Mr. Murillo was born in 1618 and was the youngest of 14 children born to Sevillian parents. At the age of 9, his father passed away and, a year later, his mother died. Murillo's brothers and sisters were much older than he and had moved away, leaving Murillo under the care of an aunt. She was married to a wealthy Sevillian doctor who ran a very strict religious household.

It was quite a change for young Bartolomé, and he suffered greatly under his uncle's rigid regime. The once happy home life that young Murillo enjoyed had been replaced by an overly stern Catholic upbringing, leading to frequent clashes with his authoritarian uncle.

In the centre of the sitting room in the doctor's house hung a huge work of art entitled Jesus the Shepherd Boy. It held a great place of pride within the doctor's heart, and he received great joy when guests would comment on this unavoidable tribute to Christ each time they came to visit.

Murillo hated this painting, as it conveyed everything he detested about his new upbringing. He despised the deadly serious looking shepherd boy that stood bolt upright, stiff and lifeless, within the golden gilt frame. He couldn't stand the shepherd staff that looked like a sentinel's bayonet in the depressing shepherd boy's hand. Worst of all, the young Murillo loathed the distinctive halo that shone down on the shepherd boy's gaunt face and perfectly clean complexion. It weakly reflected the prissy boy's rosy cheeks and brought light to his comatose and lifeless eyes. Murillo knew that no boy should ever have to look like Jesus the Shepherd Boy.

One day, while his adoptive parents were out of the house, young Bartolomé took the painting down off the wall and began to work on it with his own set of paints. The firm, resolute face of the shepherd boy was given a wide mischievous grin. His eyes were enlivened with a bright sparkle. The halo around his head soon became a scruffy straw hat. His perfect hair quickly turned into a dishevelled mop. The staff held in his hand transformed into a gnarled walking stick, and the flaccid lamb that stood by his side became a scruffy dog.

When his uncle and aunt returned home, they were in for a surprise. There, greeting them as they entered into their sitting room was a completely different Jesus the Shepherd Boy painting hanging on their wall. Disturbed by the apparent sacrilege committed by his nephew, the uncle forced young Murillo to walk the streets of Seville carrying the defaced painting in order to shame him for his blasphemous behaviour. However, his plan backfired.

In the crowd that day stood the great religious icon painter Juan Del Castillo, who was so greatly impressed by the raw talent he saw in the young upstart that he took the boy into his home as an apprentice and began to work with Murillo, teaching him the art of painting. Castillo's efforts were not in vain, and today, Bartolomé Esteban Murillo is known as one of Spain's greatest religious artists.

I believe that Bartolomé Esteban Murillo did to Jesus what we need to do as well. He freed Jesus to be all he is by giving life to the lifeless Jesus often portrayed to us by our churches. He stripped Christ of the wishy-washy-ness that we have forced upon him and clothed him with a wild mischievousness that restores the true dignity of his divine humanity. Bartolomé's uncle, like so many churches, preferred an insipid, tame Jesus, stuck as a comforting ornament on a wall to be greatly admired but whose radical mission is easily ignored. But Jesus isn't tame. He is wild, mischievous, and he is alive today.

If we perceive Jesus as "Gentle Jesus, meek and mild" then we domesticate him and thus ignore the truth of his revolutionary calling. But if we understand the true biblical Jesus as portrayed in the scriptures we cannot help but realize that Jesus came to start a revolution.

FREE THE CHILDREN, EMPOWER THE WOMEN

To describe Jesus as a radical might seem absurd to most people. Some might even point to scriptures like Mark 10, where Jesus hugged little children, or Matthew 5:39-42, where Jesus told his followers to turn the other cheek, walk the extra mile and allow people to take advantage of them as proof texts backing their argument for a non-radical Jesus.

For many, these scriptures are the evidence needed to support their view of a gentle, placid, non-revolutionary Jesus. However, when one takes a closer look at Mark 10 and Matthew 5, it becomes very clear that these gospel writers actually support a radical Jesus vastly different than the Jesus portrayed in our churches and in the many religious images we have made of him. In fact, these very scriptures are actually revolutionary texts.

Let's take a look at Mark 10:13-17:

> People were bringing little children to Jesus to have him touch them, but the disciples rebuked them. When Jesus saw this, he was indignant. He said to them, "Let the little children come to me, and do not hinder them, for the kingdom of God belongs to such as these. I tell you the truth, anyone who will not receive the kingdom of God like a little child will never enter it." And he took the children in his arms, put his hands on them and blessed them.

It is very interesting that the writer of this Gospel places this story of the children being blessed right after Jesus had preached a strong pro-marriage message against divorce and remarriage (Mk 10:2-12). In fact, Jesus message on divorce was so tough that his disciples' response to his words were "If this is the situation between a husband and a wife, it is better not to marry" (Mt 19:10).

Jesus took a hard stance against the easy divorce common in his day because it was abusive towards women and children. In Jesus' day a man could divorce his wife for basically any reason. If a man got bored of his wife, he was legally empowered to abandon her. Obviously, the fallout from this was catastrophic. Women were left alone with their fatherless children and no means to provide for themselves. This was especially troublesome in a male-dominated culture in which there was limited work available for women.

This is probably why Jesus showed so much mercy towards prostitutes. He knew that single women did not have many job opportunities to provide for themselves. This lack of opportunity for single or widowed women fuelled the sex trade.[2] By condemning this abusive but legal practice of irresponsible divorce, Jesus was protecting women and children. He was also challenging the entire male domineering culture of his day. In this, one could say that Jesus was a feminist! A truly revolutionary act that Christians everywhere must emulate.

The Matthew 19:13-15 and Mark 10:13-17 passages of children being blessed by Jesus are strategically positioned right after Jesus defended the rights of women and children by speaking against divorce. By placing these stories in this order the Gospel writers are trying to make a point about the value of women and children. By retelling this story of Jesus blessing children, they are loudly proclaiming the value of women and children to a male-dominated society that held little respect toward women and children. In fact, these writers raise the value of children by quoting Jesus' words:

> "Let the little children come to me, and do not hinder them, for the kingdom of God belongs to such as these. I tell you the truth, anyone who will not receive the kingdom of God like a little child will never enter it." And he took the children in his arms and blessed them. (Mk 10:14-16)

These were radical words and revolutionary actions. Jesus challenged the status quo of a male chauvinistic society by placing the children at a higher value than the male disciples he spoke to. His tone was intense and angry. It says that Jesus was irate with his male disciples, who had, true to form, taken on the male-dominated attitude of the day by rebuking the children as well as those who were bringing them to Jesus (their mothers?). The word *irate* means that Jesus was so angry that he saw red! The adrenaline in his body shot up a few notches when he saw how poorly his disciples were treating these children and their caregivers. The only time Jesus is recorded to be this angry was towards those who oppressed his people through religion (Mt 23) and the times that he went to the temple and fashioned a whip to drive out the money changers who were oppressing the poor (Mt 21:12-16, Mk 11:15-18) by charging them over-priced fees. All radical actions.

Then Jesus did something unspeakable. He gave all the children a great big bear hug of a blessing! This isn't a sentimental, soppy action taken on by a big softy. No, it is a ground-breaking, radical act of defiance against the way things were supposed to be. By his actions, he declared that his kingdom does not have pecking orders. In Jesus' kingdom, all are valued as important. This truth had to rankle all the men who enjoyed their powerful status over women and children. They were now facing a radical adversary who stood against them and their way of life.

SHAME THE POWER

In Matthew 5:39-41, Jesus told his followers to turn the other cheek, walk the extra mile and allow people to even strip them naked! In order to understand the revolutionary tone of Jesus' words here, it is important to understand what Jesus is saying within the context of his times.[3]

> I tell you, do not resist an evil person. If someone strikes you on the right cheek, turn to him the other also. And if someone wants to sue you and take your tunic, let him have your cloak as well. If someone forces you to go one mile, go with him two miles. (Mt 5: 39-41)

Upon a first reading of this passage, it appears that Jesus is not very revolutionary at all. But Jesus' teaching is given in the context of the struggle between his listeners and the abusive Roman powers. By sharing these three anecdotes, Jesus told his followers that injustice must not be tolerated. Moreover, he is telling his beaten-down audience to fight the power.

Jesus never taught that we are to take a non-resistant stance to any form of evil. Jesus knew that we must never ignore the reality of evil and allow it to exist without being confronted. To choose to ignore its existence or neglect to challenge it head on is sinful.

However, Jesus' method of combating evil is far different than what most people would espouse to use. When Jesus says, "Do not resist an evil person" (Mt 5:39), he uses a specific term to describe what type of resistance we are not to use. The Greek word that Matthew uses for resist is *antistenai*, which can be defined as a military term used to describe how armies would face each other, head on, in a violent clash. By using this term for resistance, Jesus is preaching against the two common responses to Roman oppression that was prevalent in his day: zealot terrorism and complete non-resistance.

Jesus did not endorse the violent acts of resistance espoused by the Zealots. These vicious freedom fighters were a para-militaristic movement known for killing Roman dignitaries and Roman soldiers through simple and quiet acts of assassination and terror. The Zealots' most popular method of violence was to use a small dagger that they would press into the flesh of Romans in crowded places. This way they could kill quickly and leave undetected. They also were known for kidnapping Roman authorities and using them as bargaining chips to free some of their own men who were imprisoned. Other times they would just kidnap and kill for revenge purposes.

Jesus taught that violent acts are not the proper way to resist evil people. He knew that the violent acts of the Zealots were not working. Violence only brought more violence upon the people of Israel by their Roman occupiers. So, if Jesus did not support violent resistance, did he endorse passive acceptance as the proper response to oppression? No, it is clear that Jesus did not support cowardly non-resistance in response to Roman subjugation. Jesus did not side with Jews too afraid to fight back, who accepted suffering as their lot in life. Fearful silence, like violent retribution, is not Jesus' way to resist evil.

Jesus never supported violence or irresponsible cowardice in the face of oppression. Martin Luther King Jr. once said, "To ignore evil is to be an accomplice to it." Jesus doesn't want his listeners to pretend evil does not exist by closing their eyes to its reality. He also does not want them to stoop as low as their oppressors and use violence as a response to the injustice they suffered.

Instead, he told them how they are to resist evil in a righteous way. Jesus proposed assertive non-violence to fight oppression through loving actions in the form of brave, peaceful, non-violent acts of protest. Jesus taught the Jews to deal with their Roman oppressors through creative forms of political resistance.

TURN THE OTHER CHEEK

"If someone strikes you on the right cheek, turn to him the other also" (Mt 5:39). To hit someone on the right cheek, it is natural to use the left hand. But in Jesus' day, the left hand was reserved for the use of unclean tasks and one was prohibited from using it to strike a person. So, the only way to hit someone on the right cheek was with the right backhand. So, a right backhand strike became the common method of treating inferiors.

This is where things get a little radical. By telling oppressed people to turn the other cheek, Jesus was empowering them to never allow themselves to be treated as an inferior. Turning the other cheek exposed the left cheek. The oppressor could not hit the exposed left cheek with a right backhand. He would have to use his right fist. And herein lies the magnificence of the protest. In Jesus' day, only equals fought with fists. By turning his left cheek, the victim forces the oppressor not to strike him, thus making himself an equal with his oppressor.

That is assertive, nonviolent protest! By turning the cheek, the person being treated as inferior declared, "I am a human just like you and I refuse to be treated unequally."

This uncomplicated but bold revolutionary statement, "If someone strikes you on the right cheek, turn to him the other also," rings true today just as it did in Jesus' day. Issues such as racism, sexism, modern-day slavery and callous labour practices are turned on their head by this one simple sentence that boldly declares equality for all people regardless of their age, sex or culture. Jesus prioritized these concerns and left us an example as revolutionary Christians to do the same.

GIVE YOUR CLOTHES AWAY

The second form of assertive non-violent action is seen in these words of Jesus: "If someone wants to sue you and take your tunic, let him have your cloak as well" (Mt 5:40).

In Jesus' day, the common people faced an economic crisis. The tax burden on the population of Israel was enormous and caused many people to seek out lenders to pay their taxes. These unscrupulous money-lenders charged ridiculous amounts of interest on their loans forcing the borrowers to be sued for not paying back their debts. This resulted in the borrower losing what little they had to the lender. Those who could not repay the lender would end up in debtors' prison.

Jesus' words, "if someone wants to sue you and take your tunic," were spoken to these poor people who had been victimized by the unjust economic system. They were the ones who could not afford to pay their debts and were being sued over their possessions, even the very tunics they wore! Jesus' response to them was to tell them to protest this injustice by giving away their cloaks as well.

If the sued party had to give up even their outer garment to pay an unjust debt, then they should also take off their under garment as well. Imagine this happening in a court of law. What a scene that would make! The person would be left naked, and this is where the protest made perfect sense as nakedness was taboo in Judaism, and shame fell less on the naked party and more on those who saw the nakedness. Through the act of stripping, the sued person brought shame on the person who was suing them, as well as upon the entire unjust judicial system. It exposed the reality that the legal system was leaving them destitute—without even the clothes on their backs.

This was one incredible, even humorous, assertive act of nonviolent protest over the injustice against the poor. Imagine how this teaching about the unjust treatment of the poor applies to our culture today, especially in the area of fair trade. Revolutionary Christians must prayerfully consider the many implications that arise from Jesus' words in this teaching, and we must act accordingly.

GO THE SECOND MILE

The third form of assertive non-violent form of protest Christ taught was, "If someone forces you to go one mile, go with him two miles" (Mt 5:41).

While on marches through conquered regions, Roman soldiers would humiliate local citizens by forcing them to carry their packs for a mile. This served two purposes. First, it gave the soldiers a break. Second, it was degrading, emphasizing to the conquered people that they were a defeated nation. By forcing Jews to carry their packs like a human mule, these soldiers utterly humiliated them. However, according to Roman law, a Roman soldier could only force a person to carry their equipment for one mile. To force someone to go an extra mile would be an infraction of military code, potentially resulting in great trouble for the offending soldier.

Now, imagine a Jew who refuses to stop after a mile. Can you picture the Roman soldier pleading with the Jew to give his pack back because he is scared that he will get in trouble for breaking Roman law? Once again, Jesus humorously makes his point: "If someone forces you to go one mile, go with him two miles." What a great way to protest injustice!

Through these teachings, Jesus empowered the exploited poor. He enabled them to see a way of resisting injustice through humour and hope, and he showed them the positive power of assertive non-violent confrontation of a system that was evil and humiliating.

I hope that at this point of the book you are beginning to see a Jesus that is more revolutionary than you previously thought. Through these verses we see Christ standing up against the powers that be by empowering the oppressed to resist the injustice they face. Add to this his bold action of taking a whip to the religious establishment at the temple, as well as the many times he confronted the religious elite, and you have one very effective radical.

No wonder he was crucified as a revolutionary.

But there is more.

WHAT DID WE EXPECT?

Jesus the Revolutionary should not surprise us. After all, his appearance was prophesied in the scriptures. This is why Palestine of Jesus' day was such a hotbed of political intrigue and rebellion. Since Israel had suffered immensely under the Roman Empire, "messiah-like" leaders often found a willing audience to join their resistance movements by referring to the many prophetic scriptures that spoke of a revolutionary messiah who would come and destroy Israel's enemies.

Now pretend you are a political leader who lived during the time of Jesus. The political climate is unstable due to the dreams of the people who are desperately seeking out possible messiahs to overturn your government and set up their own theocratic rule. Revolutionary movements are bursting through the very societal seams that you have constructed to protect you, forcing you to always look behind your back in case someone or something was about to take you out. And, you are aware of the prophecies concerning a coming king who will overthrow your authority. This was the situation King Herod faced.

Herod was an evil despot who did anything to stay in control of his throne, including murder.[4] He was aware of the biblical prophecies concerning a coming king—prophecies like:

> For to us a child is born, to us a son is given, and the government will be on his shoulders. And he will be called Wonderful Counsellor, Mighty God, Everlasting Father, Prince of Peace. Of the increase of his government and peace there will be no end. **He will reign on David's throne** and over his kingdom establishing it and upholding it with justice and righteousness from that time on and forever. **The zeal of the Lord almighty will accomplish this**. (Is 9:6-7, emphasis added)

This prophecy frightened Herod deeply because it describes, in very political terms, a new world order that the messiah would set up, a rule of God that is in total opposition to the reign of Herod.

Herod was also familiar with a prophecy that said: "The sceptre will not depart from Judah, nor the ruler's staff from between his feet, until **he comes to whom it belongs and the obedience of the nations is his**" (Gn 49:10, emphasis added).

It is for these reasons that the ever-paranoid Herod reacted so strongly when he heard about magi snooping about Jerusalem, asking, "Where is the one who has been born king of the Jews" (Mt 2:1). He called on the chief priests and teachers of the law to inquire of them where this messiah king was to be born (Mt 2:4) and was informed that it was written "But you Bethlehem, in the land of Judah...**out of you will come a ruler who will be the shepherd of my people Israel**" (Mt 2:6, emphasis added).

Worried that he would be overthrown, Herod lied to the magi (who did not go along with his manipulations, Mt 2:8-12) and eventually set in motion a holocaust by killing every boy under the age of two in Judah (Mt 2:16). But Jesus escaped Herod's wrath (Mt 2:13-15).

Do you get the point? Even as a baby, Jesus struck fear in the hearts of those in power. Herod fully knew that Jesus was a revolutionary, and it scared him to the point of irrational behaviour. His fear was not based on any coalition that Jesus had formed with other governing powers. He wasn't frightened of Jesus because of his political debonair or connections. His fear wasn't due to any human abilities that Jesus possessed. After all, in the case of Herod, Jesus was just a baby with no political influence at all, a baby that depended on his mother to feed and dress him. Yet Herod was petrified of Jesus. Why? Because Herod knew that prophetic scriptures foretold that Jesus was divinely appointed to bring about a revolution simply because he was ordained by God to be the king of kings.

How is it that an evil king could understand that Jesus was a revolutionary threat while many in the church have missed out on the revolutionary ramifications of Jesus Christ?

The Psalmist understood the revolutionary impact of Jesus. In Psalm 2:4, we read of a God who laughs at the pride of the empires of the world that boast of their great might. In opposition to these worldly regimes, God says that he has installed his own king (Ps 2:6). Then, God says to the king:

"Ask of me and I will make the nations your inheritance, the ends of the earth your possession. You will rule them with an iron sceptre; you will dash them to pieces like pottery." Therefore you kings be wise, be warned, you rulers of the earth. Serve the Lord with fear and rejoice with trembling. Kiss the son, lest he be angry and you be destroyed in your way, for his wrath can flare up in a moment. Blessed are all who take refuge in him. (Ps 2:8-12)

Later, in Psalm 72, we read:

He will defend the afflicted among the people and save the children of the needy; he will crush the oppressor…He will rule from sea to sea…All kings will bow down to him and all nations will serve him. For he will deliver the needy who cry out, the afflicted who have no one to help. He will take pity on the weak and the needy and save the needy from death. He will rescue them from oppression and violence, for precious is their blood in his sight. (Ps 72:4, 8, 11-14)

Throughout the Old Testament, we come across prophecies concerning the arrival of this revolutionary king of kings who will rule with justice and righteousness, who will defend the cause of the oppressed and take his stand against any power that dominates the poor and the weak. Yet, why have many of us missed this truth about the radical Jesus?

In the New Testament, these prophecies continue. In Luke 1, there is the famous magnificat of Mary, where she foretells the birth of Jesus as an act of God's justice on behalf of the afflicted:

My soul glorifies the Lord and my spirit rejoice sin God my saviour…He has performed mighty deeds with his arm; he has scattered those who are proud in their inmost thoughts. He had brought down rulers from thrones but has lifted up the humble. He has filled the hungry with good things but has sent the rich away empty. (Lk 1:46, 51-53)

A few verses later, Zechariah prophecies about Jesus:

Praise be to the Lord, the God of Israel, because he has come and has redeemed his people. He has raised up a horn of salvation for us in the house of his servant David (as he said through his holy prophets of long ago), salvation from our enemies and from the hand of all who hate us-to show mercy to our fathers. (Lk 1:68-72)

The word *horn* in Zechariah's prophecy is a common term used to describe power, might and kingship. Zechariah saw Jesus as the king that destroys injustice.

Biblical prophecies foretell that the coming of Jesus would set into motion a revolution of justice. Through Jesus, God is bringing about a new world order, a revolution of justice that was prophesied right up to the birth of Christ and was inaugurated through his life and formalized as a revolutionary movement upon his resurrection. The early Christians understood the divine and radical lineage of Jesus Christ. Their rebellion of love against the actions of the evil and oppressive Roman government were clearly seen in the way they lived and cared for those who were victimized by such a repressive system.

The word of God has spoken. It is time for us to destroy our safe constructs of Jesus and recapture the scriptural certainty of the revolutionary impact that Christ has in our world today.

Jesus is still the king of kings and is exalted above any force that tries to act against him and those who he fights for, the poor and oppressed. In Philippians 2:9-11, we read:

God exalted him [Jesus] to the highest place and gave him the name that is above every name, that at the name of Jesus every knee should bow, in heaven and on earth and under the earth, and every tongue confess that Jesus Christ is Lord, to the glory of God the Father.

Today, his revolution must continue through those who call themselves followers of Jesus.

Notes

[1] Michael Frost, *Exiles* (Peabody: Hendrickson Publishers, 2006), 28.

[2] The same can be said about the sex trade today. In many developing countries, poor women resort to prostitution to provide for their families. In North America, the sex trade is filled with poor women who come to the continent enticed by the oppor-

tunity of jobs so they can send money back home to their families. However, when they get here they end up being forced into stripping and/or prostitution.

3 Walter Wink, *The Powers That Be* (New York: DoubleDay, 1998).

4 Herod was a man very familiar with murder. He had his first wife and mother-in-law murdered. He also butchered all of his sons born to him from his first wife and had his brother-in-law executed. He burned alive a number of Jewish leaders. Most, if not all, of these killings were done to secure his throne. Herod was treacherous in weeding out any sniff of an overthrow of his reign, and he stopped at nothing to secure his throne.

PART TWO

THE SECRET LIFE OF A JESUS REVOLUTIONARY

"We must see and know Christ before we can teach."

Mary Slessor

"The greatest challenge of the day is how to bring about a revolution of the heart, a revolution which has to start with each one of us."

Dorothy Day (Catholic activist)

"What do you possess if you possess not God?"

Saint Augustine

"I like your Christ; I do not like your Christians. You Christians are so unlike your Christ."

Mahatma Ghandi

"We are called in our lives as sons and daughters of God to dare to imitate divine perfection—to be participators of the divine nature. Our supernatural birthright, lost to us in Eden, was restored in the blood of the Saviour on Calvary."

Samuel Cardinal Stritch (Archbishop of Chicago)

"Christ in you the hope of glory."

Apostle Paul

CHAPTER FIVE

THE NEED FOR THE HOLY SPIRIT: THE POWER OF THE JESUS REVOLUTION

In the first section of this book, we discovered that Jesus came to start a revolutionary movement of love, not the stifling, compliantly docile religion that is far too prevalent in our world today. The Gospel accounts show us that everything that opposed life was in the crosshairs of this Jesus revolution. To Jesus, poverty, racism, economic disparity, violence, classism, sexism and all other forms of injustice and oppression must never be tolerated in the revolutionary kingdom reign of God. Jews and Gentiles, slaves and freepersons, men and women, children and adults are all to be honoured as possessing equal value as children of God.

Any form of oppressive systemic control that took advantage of people was anathema to the Jesus revolution, and it must be the same today. Oppression and injustice is alive and well in our day and it forces us to ask: Are we willing to continue in the revolutionary path of Jesus and labour on behalf of the oppressed of our day, no matter what the personal cost? Or, will we go the way of the religious institution and blindly walk our way through a world of need?

This is the question that Oscar Romero had to face while serving Christ in Central America during the volatile 1980s. At that time, the people of El Salvador were suffering at the blood-stained hands of an American-supported military dictatorship. Against the totalitarian regime, whose actions led to masses of malnourished children, vast human rights violations and assassinations of the opposition, a large number of Catholic clergy sided with the oppressed poor. On February 23, 1977, Oscar Romero providentially entered the scene and became the archbishop of San Salvador, a move that was welcomed by the corrupt government but greatly opposed by the priests serving the rural poor. To these activist priests, Oscar Romero was an extremely timid, conservative man with a history of non-involvement in the plight of the oppressed of his country. To his critics, Romero was a coward, a weak man whose appointment was made to placate the oppressive regime.

However, two weeks after his instalment as archbishop, Oscar Romero faced his first crisis. His good friend, Jesuit Priest Rutilio Grande, was assassinated by the military regime while working with the rural peasants. His murder forced Romero to face the reality of the great social injustice happening all around him. Awakened through the tragedy of personal loss, the newly installed archbishop visited the impoverished coffee plantation workers and was sickened by what he saw. The brazen abuse that these labourers endured at the hands of the rich landowners was unconscionable. He became indignant that over 65 percent of the local peasants were landless while only 14 controlling families possessed over 60 percent of the arable land in his diocese.

Upon visiting with the poor of his land, Oscar Romero gradually became a strong spokesperson for the powerless, speaking out against social injustice, torture, assassinations and the stifling poverty that his people endured. The archbishop couldn't help but give legitimacy to the mission of his priests, and he joined in their work on behalf of the poor.

It didn't take long for the establishment to take notice. They quickly took action regarding Romero's blatant disregard for their repressive policies, and graffiti began to appear in the archbishop's diocese of San Salvador: "Be a patriot, kill a priest." On March 24, 1980, Oscar Romero was assassinated while performing the Holy Eucharist, his blood symbolically spilling out onto the altar. His murder took place a day after he had publically called on all Christian Salvadorian soldiers to obey God's higher order and stop being part of the tyrannical governmental system that was using their powers to kill and oppress people.

Oscar Romero's commitment to Christ forced him to leave a safe institutionalized religion that passively ignored injustice to follow Jesus' revolutionary path. By doing this, he was a true follower of Jesus involved in enacting the kingdom of God in El Salvador. In a sermon he gave shortly before his death, Romero said:

I am going to speak to you simply as a pastor, as one who, together with his people, has been learning the beautiful but harsh truth that the Christian faith does not cut us off from the world but immerses us in it; the church is not a fortress set apart from the city. The church follows Jesus, who lived, worked, struggled and died in the midst of a city, in the polis. It is in this sense that I should like to talk about the political dimension of the Christian faith: in the precise sense of the repercussions of faith on the world and also of the repercussions that being in the world has on faith.[1]

THE PLACE OF THE HOLY SPIRIT IN THE JESUS REVOLUTION

The Holy Spirit was the driving force in the life of Oscar Romero and was essential in providing him with the conviction and power to stand up against all forms of evil (Jn 16:7-15).

This is the secret power that filled Romero. He acted on the impulse of the Holy Spirit in opposing the atrocities that were happening in his community. As a deeply spiritual man of prayer, he took Jesus seriously, so it should not surprise us that God would call him to be Jesus to the poor of El Salvador.

The same Holy Spirit that was in Oscar Romero is the same Spirit of the Lord that inhabited the revolutionary Jesus Christ. "The Spirit of the Lord is upon me, because he has anointed me to preach good news to the poor. He has sent me to proclaim freedom for the prisoners and recovery of sight for the blind, to release the oppressed, to proclaim the year of the Lord's favour" (Lk 4:18-19).

Romero is a good example that true followers of Jesus cannot help but be radicals in a world of injustice. This is because the Holy Spirit in Jesus and in Oscar Romero is the same Holy Spirit in all of us who claim Christ as lord. It is the Holy Spirit of God that awakens our conscience of the presence of evil and then empowers and emboldens us to be conveyors of an alternative reality—the just, peaceful and loving kingdom of God. This is why Jesus, after his resurrection, breathed the Holy Spirit into the apostles. "Jesus said, 'Peace be with you! **As the Father has sent me, I am sending you.**' And with that he breathed on them and said, '**Receive the Holy Spirit**'" (Jn 20:21-22, emphasis added).

It is interesting that Jesus gave the apostles the Holy Spirit just before his ascension when he commissioned them to do the exact same mission that he was sent to do: "As you sent me into the world, I have sent them into the world" (Jn 17:18). This is the way of Jesus. His mission is our mission, and his kingdom of God cause must be our cause. Jesus gives us the Holy Spirit because the only way we can live like Jesus is through a life that is activated by the Holy Spirit inside of us. There is no other way.

This is why Jesus said:

> Unless I go away, the Counsellor will not come to you; but if I go, I will send him to you. But when he, the Spirit of truth, comes, **he will guide you into all truth.** He will not speak on his own; he will speak only what he hears, and he will tell you what is yet to come. He will bring glory to me by taking from what is mine and making it known to you. (Jn 16:7,13-15, emphasis added)

The Holy Spirit invigorates us to be people of God's kingdom rule on earth.

STAGES OF THE HOLY SPIRIT

After Jesus breathed the Holy Spirit into the apostles, he instructed them to wait on the Lord to fill (baptize) them with the Holy Spirit:

> Do not leave Jerusalem, but wait for the gift my Father promised, which you have heard me speak about. For John baptized with water but in a few days **you will be baptized with the Holy Spirit...You will receive power when the Holy Spirit comes on you**; and **you will be my witnesses in Jerusalem**, and in all of Judea and Samaria, and to the ends of the earth. (Acts 1:4-5,8, emphasis added)

Notice the process? First, they are to wait for the filling of the Holy Spirit. Then, they are to go and do Spirit-infused mission. The link between the Holy Spirit and our missional action is very important if we are to live as radical Christians. In other words there is a need for an infilling of the Holy Spirit before we have the power to act like Jesus. Mission is not about us doing God's work; it is about God doing his work through us to accomplish his mission in the world.

To be like Jesus is impossible. Though we cherish and appreciate Jesus' teaching about love and peace, we have to admit that we have a hard time actually doing what Jesus did and obeying his words to us! It is easy to be familiar with the words of Jesus. Anyone can open up a Bible and read the Gospels, but we need more, so much more. We need to do the words of Jesus, and this means that we desperately need the power of the Holy Spirit activated in us so that we can live out the words of Jesus!

None of us can live like Jesus on our own strength. When we realize this we will give up trying to act like Jesus. This is actually good. It knocks us to our knees and causes us to cry out to God for his help to live like Christ. It is in this act of surrender that the Holy Spirit comes in; he is the source that empowers us to live like Christ.

The apostles are examples of people who lived surrendered lives. They obeyed Jesus and gathered together in an upper room in Jerusalem, where they spent their time praying and waiting on the Holy Spirit to fill them. Sure enough, a great wind blew through that place and each one of them were baptized in the Holy Spirit.

> When the day of Pentecost came, they were all together in one place. Suddenly a sound like the blowing of a violent wind came from heaven and filled the whole house where they were sitting. They saw what seemed to be tongues of fire that separated and came to rest on each of them. **All of them were filled with the Holy Spirit** and began to speak in other tongues as the Spirit enabled them. (Acts 2:1-4, emphasis added)

The question must be asked, Why did they get baptized in the Holy Spirit? After all, they already had the Holy Spirit through Jesus breathing it into them before the Pentecost experience (Jn 20:21-22). But here we read that they are filled with the Holy Spirit afterwards, during the Pentecost experience.

From this, we learn that Jesus gives the Holy Spirit to every believer. The Holy Spirit dwells in us when we become Christians through our faith in Christ. In this way, we have the Spirit of God in us, but do we have the fullness of the power of the Spirit in us? Jesus **breathed the Spirit into his disciples, giving them the potential to be filled with the Spirit** of God. On Pentecost, the Spirit that dwelt in them, through Jesus breathing on them, filled them. Thus, there seems to be stages of infilling of the Holy Spirit.

Perhaps this is why Romero started off as a faint-hearted follower of Jesus in the midst of maddening injustice. Though he had the Holy Spirit in him, he remained compliant with the oppressive powers that be. This relates to us as well. Why are so many Christians in the Western world silent regarding atrocities that our governments commit against poorer nations? Are we not like the pre-activist Romero? In the shrinking global village that we live in today, we are made aware of injustice all around us, but yet we choose to ignore the cries of the poor. Shouldn't it bother us when our nation uses unfair trade practices, military embargoes or violent intervention in order to get what we want? Or that children dodge bullets in housing projects and others live and die on our inner-city streets? Our callous ignorance testifies to our need to be filled with the Holy Spirit. Yes, we might have the Holy Spirit in us and we might even feel a little bit of conviction regarding the evil all around us, but are we filled with the Holy Spirit? Only the infilling of the Spirit of God can break us free from our naturally selfish desires so that we become animated with the love of Christ towards those around us.

PRACTICAL IMPLICATIONS OF THE INFILLING OF THE HOLY SPIRIT

Acts 2:1-4 teaches four important principles the apostles practiced that opened their hearts to the infilling of the Spirit of God. First of all, the apostles already had the Spirit of God as followers of Christ. Christ had breathed the Holy Spirit into them; the Spirit was alive as a seed just waiting to bloom in the lives of the apostles. Secondly, the apostles were willing to venture out in mission for Jesus. They knew that they were to be witnesses[2] on behalf of Jesus and his cause. The enormity of this task humbled them into dependence on God for his indwelling Spirit. Thirdly, they were obedient to Christ. They followed Jesus' instruction to go Jerusalem for the infilling of his Spirit. This was an enormous act of obedience, as Jerusalem housed the religious authorities that had condemned their revolutionary leader to death. Fourthly, they waited on God and prayed. They acknowledged their desperate need for the fullness of the Holy Spirit and demonstrated their need for him by prayerfully waiting on God to give them his infilling.

By doing these things, the apostles demonstrated that the Holy Spirit will not hold back from those who desperately seek his fullness.

Interestingly, right after they were filled with the Holy Spirit, the apostles immediately went forth in mission. This small, fearful band of Jesus followers, led by Peter, who had denied even knowing Jesus three times during his trial (Lk 22:54-62), was transformed into bold and powerful revolutionaries. Peter, the great denier, even preached to a multitude of people right after his infilling of the Holy Spirit. This once terrified follower who denied Christ boldly spoke publically to thousands of people. This is what the Holy Spirit does. His filling provides us with the divine energy to fulfill the mission Christ bestows upon us.

Peter's message was simple:

> God has made this Jesus, whom you crucified, both Lord and Christ. Repent and be baptized every one of you, in the name of Jesus Christ, so that your sins may be forgiven. And **you will receive the gift of the Holy Spirit**...With many other words he warned them; "Save yourselves from this corrupt generation." (Acts 2:36,38,40, emphasis added)

What a message Peter gave that day. Over three thousand people were saved![3] This means that three thousand men had turned away from their personal involvement in an evil, unjust society to embrace a new kingdom with Jesus as their king.

And something else happened—they also received the same Holy Spirit that radicalized Jesus and the apostles.

The same infilling of the Holy Spirit that infused the early church is available for us today. As Dr. Tony Campolo says:

> Jesus saved us in order that He might begin to transform His world into the kind of world that He willed for it to be when He created it. When Jesus saved us, He saved us to be agents of a great revolution, the end of which will come when the kingdoms of this world will become the Kingdom of our God.

The commonality among Jesus, the apostles and the early church was the fullness of the Holy Spirit. This same infilling of the Spirit transformed Oscar Romero into a revolutionary for the kingdom of God, and it can radicalize us. When we open our hearts to the Holy Spirit, we can be transformed as well. Without the Spirit overflowing in us, we will never accomplish God's revolutionary will for our lives.

NOTES

[1] Marie Dennis, Renny Golden and Scott Wright, *Oscar Romero: Reflections on His Life and Writing* (Maryknoll: Orbis Books 2000), 16-17.

[2] The word for witness in the ancient Greek means martyr, a suitable term to describe revolutionaries.

[3] It is likely that more than three thousand people were saved, as women and children would not have been included in the number that Luke states.

CHAPTER SIX

LOVE OF GOD: THE MOTIVATION OF THE JESUS REVOLUTION

"I began a revolution with 82 men. If I had to do it again, I'd do it with 10 or 15 and absolute faith. It does not matter how small you are if you have faith and a plan of action."

Fidel Castro

Contrary to what most of us think, revolutions are not anchored and sustained by zealous leadership, dazzling oratory or stubborn, political willpower. The gifts and abilities of the radicals involved in a revolution are not what make a revolution effective. Believe it or not, the key distinguishing attribute that births and sustains revolution is love. Che Guevara once said, "At the risk of sounding ridiculous, let me say that the true revolutionary is guided by feelings of love." The foundational mechanism that drives revolution is love, a love for people, a love for justice, a love for country, a love for freedom and yes, in worst-case scenarios, a love of power.

The Jesus revolution is no different. We, as Jesus revolutionaries, must be fired up by love. Not a love for power or even a love for justice for the oppressed, but a deep, passionate love for Jesus. Jesus commands us: "Love the Lord your God with all your heart and with all your soul and with all your strength and with all your mind; and Love your neighbour as yourself" (Lk 10:27). One of the greatest fears I have with radical Christianity is that it can attract people who are either looking for a program that supports their negative reaction against the religious right or a justification for their rebellion against how modern-day or traditional church is done. I would hate to see Jesus' revolutionary purposes stalled because people have joined in a spirit of protest as a tool to propel their own political agenda or aspirations for social causes. If this happens, the movement will become human led, not Spirit led.

In contrast, Jesus' revolution must be birthed in our souls by a hunger for Jesus Christ, as opposed to being a response from angry, self-proclaimed prophets. The Jesus movement must be concerned with recapturing the heart and soul of the early Christians, which is to love Christ. If our hearts' motivation is driven by a deep desire to love Jesus, we will soon be led by the Spirit to serve in our world. With the love of Christ dwelling in us and the power of the Holy Spirit working through us, we will have hearts that break over the things that break the heart of Jesus.

And, we will soon realize this important truth: if you target social problems in order to change them, you will never have the power to bring about lasting transformation. Only Jesus can bring about long-term societal change. Thus, the focus of our lives must be on our love relationship with Christ, as it will open our hearts to his Spirit and supernaturally cause us to love our neighbours. When this happens, we cannot help but be involved in social justice issues.

Jesus Christ was a social transformer simply because of his love relationship with the Father. The early church followed suit. These early Christians didn't change their world by targeting the problems present within their society. They didn't hold political rallies or devise radical strategies to protest the many injustices present in their culture.[1] Instead, they chose to focus on Jesus.

As a result, they became his loving instruments of change within their culture.

Jesus commanded us to "**Love one another. As I have loved you**, so you must love one another. All men will know you are my disciples if you love one another" (Jn 13:34-35, emphasis added). Humanly speaking, this commandment is impossible for us to fulfill. How can we love others as Christ loves us? There is only one way. The only way we can love others as Christ does is to allow the love of Jesus to fill our souls, and this can only happen in accordance with our own love for Christ.

I remember hearing about a priest who was apprehended by Roman soldiers during the early years of the church. A rumour had spread throughout a small rural town that the local priest possessed a vast array of hidden treasure. Upon hearing this claim, a group of soldiers went out to capture the priest and steal all his riches. When the soldiers arrested the priest, they forced him to take them to his secret treasure lair that was hidden in a nearby cave. When they entered the secret treasury, the priest declared loudly to his captors, "Behold, the Lord's treasure!" Before them were hundreds of poor, sick and elderly people, all living under the care of the loving priest.

This story illustrates the fact that our love of God cannot help but overflow into a love for others, especially towards those who have been marginalized by the rest of society. The Apostle Paul stated, "For Christ's love compels us…" (2 Cor 5:14). The love of Christ inside of us naturally induces loving actions towards others, both by preaching the good news of salvation through Christ alone as well as through acts of compassion. After all, this is exactly how Jesus lived while on earth. Christ was the embodiment of love, and he now lives his love through us, in the power of the Holy Spirit.

Jesus' loving actions were visibly evident in the lives of the early Christians who rescued babies left out to die on garbage heaps in Roman cities. These early Christians were the first pro-life group that ever existed. However, their belief in life was not just a political issue for them. They welcomed these babies into their homes as their own children. Jesus' love was alive in these early pro-life Christians, who also took in the sick and dying, provided for the poor and hungry and avoided all forms of military service that benefitted the abusive Roman Empire. Their loving relationship with Jesus naturally overflowed from within them.

RADICAL ACTIONS FROM LOVERS OF CHRIST

Ancient church legend tells a story of a wealthy merchant who travelled through the Mediterranean world in search of the Apostle Paul. By means of great persistence, the merchant was able to contact Timothy and a meeting was arranged. On a bright sunny day, the wealthy merchant stepped inside a dark and dirty, rat-infested jail cell in Rome, where he was surprised to be greeted by a frail-looking old man. The merchant thought to himself, "Surely this cannot be the great Paul I have heard so much about." But, as they talked, the merchant was challenged by the wisdom, tranquillity and magnetism of the elderly Paul. They spoke for hours. Finally, and sadly, he bid his farewell to this old and wise man, but only after he had begged Paul for a blessing. As the merchant left Paul's filthy jail cell, he was met by Timothy and asked, "What is the secret of this man's power? I have never encountered anything like it before."

"Do you not know? Did you not guess?" replied Timothy. "Paul is in love."

"In love?" repeated the merchant, confused by Timothy's answer.

"Yes," Timothy responded, "Paul is in love with Jesus Christ."

The merchant looked even more taken aback and responded, "Is that all?"

Smiling, Timothy replied, "Sir, that is everything."

WILLLIAM WILBERFORCE

If a revolutionary Jesus movement is to flourish it can only succeed in correspondence with our love for Jesus. We see this principle at work in the lives of the great Christian social reformers of our time. One such hero is William Wilberforce.

For over 58 years, Wilberforce fought valiantly for the abolition of slavery. His battle was a prolonged struggle that brought victory only the day before he died. What was the force that empowered William Wilberforce to tirelessly fight the injustice of slavery for 58 years, even at enormous personal cost? What was it that made William Wilberforce to stick with his convictions, even if it meant the loss of friends, influence, status and riches? His love of Jesus.

When you love Christ above power, fame, riches and personal popularity, you are free from the controlling influences of your ego that desperately seeks out these things. William Wilberforce stayed true to his calling to eliminate the slave trade not out of personal stubbornness but because he was empowered by the Spirit of God that flowed from his deep relationship with Jesus. Wilberforce's love of Christ compelled him to share this love to a group of abused and oppressed people.

MOTHER TERESA

Many of the great Catholic saints loved Jesus with such a passion and, as God's vessels, made the world a much better place. Mother Teresa of Calcutta was such a saint. She spent hours of devoted contemplation in the presence of her greatest love, Jesus. In fact, she saw her whole life and ministry as an act of contemplation.

Evangelist and modern-day contemplative Leighton Ford tells the story of his visit with Mother Teresa at her Sisters of Mercy site, in Calcutta:

> We talked about the dying poor with whom she and the sisters
> ministered as they were brought in from the streets of that

teeming city to live out their final days. Many lay on pallets near us as we spoke. "How do you keep going," I asked, "with so much poverty and pain all around?" "We do our work for Jesus and with Jesus and to Jesus," she answered, "and that's what keeps it simple. It's not a matter of praying sometimes and working others. We pray the work." She also told us how she and the other sisters sought to see Christ in the face of each one they served. I went away from that brief encounter more than strangely moved. Years later, at a prayer breakfast in Washington D.C., I heard her say, "Don't misunderstand our work. We are not social workers. We do social work. But we are contemplatives in the midst of life."[2]

For Mother Teresa, Jesus was everything. Her life purpose was to see and worship Christ in everything, everyone, everywhere, all the time. She was single-mindedly in love. Mother Teresa loved Christ so much she wanted to spend all her time in his loving presence, and it was her fond desire to be with Jesus that led her to spend her time with the poor. Why was this? Because, as Mother Teresa discovered, Jesus is most often revealed in the distressing disguise of the poor. Mother Teresa's love for Jesus led her to see Jesus revealed in the lives of the poor, the sick and the dying.

St. Augustine once said, "Love God and do whatever you want." He understood that when you love God deeply, everything you desire will lead you to godly acts. When you love God, you cannot help but love all mankind, rich and poor, oppressed and oppressor, with the love of God inside of you.

JOHN WESLEY

The great revivalist John Wesley also lived a life of loving devotion to Christ. As a child, Wesley was greatly influenced by the spirituality of his mother, Susanna, an avid reader of the great Spanish mystics St. John of the Cross and St. Teresa of Avila. As Wesley grew older, he wandered astray from his mother's virtuous ways. However, all of this changed when Wesley was caught in a horrible storm on his way from England to the United States. Aboard his ship were a group of Moravian Christians, who exhibited an extraordinary calmness and loving faith in Christ amidst the panic of the storm. Their faith in Christ became the spiritual turning point in his life, eventually leading to his salvation.

John Wesley soon possessed a great love for Jesus, a love that drove him to spend hours in prayer, Bible reading and meditation. The following quotes taken from his journal reveal his passionate love for Christ, as seen in how he longed for Jesus every second of his life. On May 25, 1738, Wesley wrote: "The moment I awaked, 'Jesus, master' was in my heart and in my mouth; and I found all my strength lay in keeping my eye fixed on him, and my soul waiting on him continually."[3] Two days later, he wrote of the joy he has in spending time with his love, Jesus Christ: "Believing one reason of my want of joy was want of time of prayer, I resolved to do no business till I went to church in the morning, but to continue pouring out my heart before him."[4]

Wesley's legacy has impacted our world by historic proportions. He was consumed with knowing and loving Christ, and this holy ambition naturally led to his powerful preaching and actions of social justice, especially on behalf of the poor. Wesley was a leader in the abolitionism movement and very active in fighting for prison reform. He was instrumental in developing schools and orphanages. His advocacy and love for the poor often pitted him against the established church, and it eventually resulted in his founding of the Methodist movement. On the tombstone of John Wesley lies this quote: "Lord, let me not live to be useless." His life's impact on our world today is a stunning testimony of what happens when we single-mindedly love Jesus.

MARTIN LUTHER KING JR. AND THE CIVIL RIGHTS MOVEMENT

The partnership between loving God and loving others was also visibly evident in the civil rights movement of the 50s and 60s. What made this movement so powerful was the fact that it was infused, first and foremost, by a deep love for Jesus Christ.

The divine anointing to bring about social justice could never have resulted from their own strength and abilities. It came from the Spirit of God that dwelt in their innermost being. Armed with a love for Christ, they knew, deep in their hearts, that their cause was ordained by God. With this truth profoundly embedded deep within their souls, they were able stare their racist opposition in the eye, even in the midst of water cannons, vicious dogs and riot police batons.

Dr. Walter Fluker, executive director of the Leadership Centre, Morehouse College, Atlanta, Georgia, tells a story of when Howard Thurman, the great African American pastor and mentor to Martin Luther King Jr., once met with him at a crucial time in his life. His words tell us much about the foundation needed for anyone of us to be effective as socially transformative Christians. Fluker recounts:

> He was a very, very intimate and caring person. And at a very private moment, he asked me what I was going to do with my life. I later discovered this was what he asked everyone. I said, "Well, I'm thinking about seminary. Beyond seminary, I'm thinking about ordained ministry. I'm thinking about maybe getting a Ph.D." I went on and on and on. And he said, "But what do you really want to do?" And I said, "I'd like to see the church really engaged in society, finding ways in which you change the world." And he looked at me for a long time, very intimately (his voice was so soft and reassuring; I hate to romanticize, but it was just so soothing), and he said, "Young man, all social issues are temporary and brief. Go deep." I hadn't the slightest idea what he meant. All I knew was that the ground shifted.[5]

After years of serving the poor in high-risk neighbourhoods, I know exactly what Dr. Howard Thurman meant. It is the depth of my love relationship with God that matters most. It is the true power source that works in me that allows me to be an agent for any real social transformation to occur. As Jesus said, "Apart from me you can do nothing" (Jn 15:5). Go Deep!

URBANPROMISE TORONTO

I work for a great ministry called UrbanPromise Toronto[6] that serves children, youth and their mothers in high-risk inner-city communities in Toronto. One of the most effective things we do is the very innovative StreetLeader program, in which we hire community youth to be after-school tutors and summer camp counsellors to the children we work with. For many of these StreetLeaders, it is their first paying job. Because of this, we have them go through leadership and job training. It is a wonderful program that has enhanced the self-esteem of our youth, as they proudly receive pay cheques for making a difference in their communities.

This visible and monetary recognition of their value has given our StreetLeaders the self confidence they need to be able to say no to the abundant temptation of drugs, gangs and promiscuous sexual behaviour that is ever present in the urban milieu. These young people understand that as leaders, they are vital role models to the children they work with. One of the greatest joys for me is when these young people graduate high school and head off to college or university. This is a very important moment in their lives, as most of them are the first in their families to graduate from post-secondary school and attend a college or university.

It costs money to run a successful ministry like our StreetLeader program. Funding must come from individuals, churches, businesses and even government coffers to help us hire marginalized youth. Needless to say, I am often in hot pursuit of the needed resources our StreetLeaders require, and this often leads me to some very interesting encounters.

I'll never forget the day I met with a political bureaucrat to ask for financial support. At the time of the meeting, our government had set aside funding for social programs involved in at-risk neighbourhoods in our city. My staff and I jumped at this opportunity, knowing full well that we met every requirement needed to receive funding. We had written a solid application to the government outlining our StreetLeader program, including documentation of the tremendous successes we have had over the years. Our proposal was so good that we received notification informing us that we had been accepted to participate in the final stages of the granting process. This final hurdle involved a lengthy interview with a funding representative from the government. As we entered into this final interview stage, we were confidently excited over our chances of receiving funding. If this interview went well, we would be the recipient of a very generous grant that would allow us to hire community youth as StreetLeaders for three years.

The interview was a disaster. The governmental consultant told us that our proposal was flawless and that we possessed everything required to receive funding, but we were being rejected because we were a Christian organization. The reasoning behind our denial was that the government did not want to be seen as favouring a religious group and, in the words of the interviewer, "they did not want to discriminate against others by accepting a Christian organization for government grants."

At this point of the interview I figured that I had nothing to lose, so I decided to play hardball with this government representative. I said: "You make no sense. You claim to be a non-discriminatory association, yet you are discriminating against us because we are Christians. You are, by your very actions, extremely discriminatory. Not only are you prejudiced against us, but you are also discriminating against every child, young person and mother we serve, many of whom are not Christians in the least."

Then I asked her, "Would you have supported Martin Luther King Jr. and the civil rights movement of the 1960s?"

Taken aback by my brazen approach, she haughtily replied, "Of course I would."

"No, you wouldn't," I replied. "Martin Luther King Jr. was a Baptist minister. He worked for a Christian organization, and you said that you would not support Christian organizations."

Pressing my luck, I continued by asking her if she would have supported William Wilberforce and his fight for the abolition of slavery. Once again she responded in the affirmative. I answered back, "Well, Wilberforce was a Christian who belonged to a Christian organization that you wouldn't have supported because you don't discriminate."

Gaining confidence, I began to rhyme off the many other great acts of historic social justice spurred on by Christians. I then asked her "Would you have supported movements such as the anti-child labour and women's suffrage movements or the anti-apartheid movement in South Africa?"

Again she answered, "Of course I would!"

"How about the organizing of hospitals and schools?"

"Yes, I would," she replied.

"How about social agencies that feed and clothe the poor like World Vision and the Salvation Army?"

At this point she knew where I was going with my questions and she also realized that I had forced her into very tough dilemma. The double standards of the government she represented had become very evident to her when confronted with the fact that Christian organizations are a force for social good. I then challenged her: "What would happen, if all the Christian social agencies in our city were to go on strike for one day? What would happen to our city if there were no more Christian-based food and clothing banks, homeless shelters, hospitals, after-school tutoring and camp programs, job training and counselling initiatives?"

She responded by admitting that the city would be in chaos. Then, I activated my secret weapon. I had three of our mothers enter the room and introduced them to the government representative by saying, "This lady represents the provincial government, and she has just told me that they will not give us money to employ your children to work with us as StreetLeaders because we are a Christian organization. What do you think of that?"

Some might think it cruel to put the poor government worker on the spot. However, I wanted this woman and the government she represented to see what their prejudiced policies were doing. It was time to make this governmental bureaucrat look into the eyes of the people most affected by their isolated and out-of-touch bureaucracy. My desperate move paid off. The atmosphere in the room electrified. These mothers couldn't believe that their government was so narrow-minded. They got angry, passionately telling my guest how UrbanPromise had transformed their lives. They spoke lovingly of their sons and daughters and how they have been given purpose and meaning because they have a job as a StreetLeader at UrbanPromise. They spoke on behalf of their children, as only mothers can, and it was obvious that my guest, a mother herself, was deeply impacted by their words.

When the meeting was over, I walked the government official to her car and thanked her for taking the time to come out and visit with us. In the back of my mind, I thought that I would never hear from this woman again.

I was wrong. The very next day I received a phone call. She told me that she was impressed by what she saw and heard about UrbanPromise and, to her credit, she pushed her authorities to accept us as one of the organizations that would receive government funding. We now had a sizable amount of funding for our StreetLeader program in recognition of the effectiveness of our work with at-risk youth.

LOVE OF GOD IS SEEN IN REVOLUTIONARY ACTS

It is true: the church has done some appalling things in the name of Jesus. But the true church, those who through their love of God are filled by his Spirit, have always been leaders for social change against injustice. We mustn't sell ourselves short. True Christians are lovers of Jesus who cannot help but make a difference in our world. The wonderful saints of the past and the present have left us a glorious legacy. They teach us to live our lives, first and foremost, from the foundation of our love relationship with Jesus Christ. This is what Howard Thurman meant when he said, "Go deep." And these great social reformers illustrate the truth of the commandment to "Love the Lord your God with all your heart and with all your soul and with all your mind. This is the first and greatest commandment. And the second is like it: Love your neighbour as yourself" (Mt 22:37-39).

Love of neighbour can only come about when we love God first. Jesus said, "For out of the overflow of the heart the mouth speaks. The good man brings good things out of the good stored up in him, and the evil man brings evil things out of the evil stored up in him" (Mt 12:34-35).

Effective societal transformation can only come about through the Spirit of God, as he works through us, from the inside out. Or, as I once read from a Starbucks bathroom wall, "The deeper the roots, the higher the reach."

It all starts with our love for Jesus.

NOTES

[1] I don't disagree with political protests as an act of love by today's standards. However, I desire to stress the importance of loving Jesus over and above having a political agenda. Jesus must be the impetus of everything we do.

[2] Leighton Ford, *The Attentive Life* (Downers Grove: InterVarsity Press, 2008), 131-132.

[3] John Wesley, *John Wesley: A Representative Collection of His Writings* ed. Albert C. Outler (Oxford: Oxford University Press, 1980), 67.

[4] Ibid.

[5] Robert Franklin, "Interview with Walter Fluker" in *Religion and Ethics* Jan 18 2002.

[6] The mission of UrbanPromise Toronto is to create shalom in government housing communities by joining children, youth and single mothers in experiencing the love of Christ. UrbanPromise also operates in Camden, New Jersey; Wilmington, Delaware; Vancouver, B.C., Honduras and Malawi, Africa.

CHAPTER SEVEN

MYSTICS: SPIRIT-FILLED REVOLUTIONARIES

"We are called in our lives as sons and daughters of God to dare to imitate divine perfection—to be participators of the divine nature. Our supernatural birthright, lost to us in Eden, was restored in the blood of the Saviour on Calvary."[1]

Samuel Cardinal Stritch (Catholic Archbishop of Chicago)

One day, St. Francis of Assisi was lost in prayer as he sat among the ruins of an old, abandoned church. While in the depths of contemplation, sitting among the strewn bricks of the dilapidated building, he had a mystical moment. He heard the voice of God tell him to rebuild the church. With his friends, St. Francis slowly rebuilt the decrepit church in which he was praying. Upon completion, he took it upon himself to restore other crumbling churches and edifices. Years later, St. Francis realized he had misunderstood his calling from Jesus to rebuild his church. Francis gradually recognized that the rebuilding process he was to be involved in was deeper and more far-reaching than brick and mortar. He became convinced that his command from Jesus to "rebuild my church" meant restoring the original purpose behind the church. God wanted Francis to strip the church of its religiosity and formality and restore it to a Jesus movement. Thus, the Franciscans were born, and Francis organized them to be a community of Jesus followers committed to a life of prayer, environmental care, peacemaking and service to the poor and destitute.

I love this story of St. Francis and the rebuilding of the church because it is a great illustration of Jesus' true intention for the church. Jesus never intended to start a religion or denomination. Denominations, mega-churches and religious rites were never on his agenda. Jesus had much larger goals. It was his intention to start a simple, subversive, life-giving, spiritual, social movement that would bring about his kingdom rule into the day-to-day happenings of the present world system. This movement would share the good news of the lordship reign of Jesus as it served the poor, broken-hearted and marginalized people ignored by the powers that be. This is the true church—to love God and people (especially the poor), over and above church buildings, religious rituals and materialistic folly.

St. Francis was a radical Christian. He was devoted to living out the words of Jesus and thus is the perfect example of what Jesus' revolutionary movement must look like. His life illustrates two important principles of the Jesus revolution. First, there is a need for mysticism in the movement. St. Francis was a mystic. His passionate love of Jesus enabled him to receive divine power to live out the very words of Christ. Everything Francis did, his love for the poor, care for the sick and boldness to risk his life to speak to an entire Muslim army came from his mystic heart of God. It was God's Spirit working through him that enabled Francis to accomplish incredible acts of peace and justice.[2]

The second lesson we learn from St. Francis is that we must be careful as mystics. Francis was told "rebuild my church," but he misinterpreted the instruction. If St. Francis had wise spiritual counsel and accountability, he would have been better able to discern what God had intended for him to do.

Unfortunately, Christian mysticism is something that we don't hear much about these days. The new age movement has hijacked this term by claiming mysticism belongs only to them. In reality, these modern-day mystics are charlatans. Because of this, many Christians tend to shy away from mysticism. Yet, mysticism has been a very important tenet of our Christian faith for centuries. In fact, in the early church, it was expected that all Christians be mystics.

One of the best ways I can describe Christian mysticism is by referring to mystical encounters I had with God while in Maui Memorial Hospital.[3] These spiritual experiences were the culmination of a period of incredible suffering. In the short span of nine months, I had suffered three terrible losses. A young man from our StreetLeader program was murdered. Then, a few months after his death, a little child drowned during a day camp outing involving my staff. I was devastated by these two great losses and went away on a sabbatical to recover from the trauma I had endured as the result from these two tragedies. I desperately desired Christ to fill me with his divine touch.

On the second day of my sabbatical, I was paralyzed from the neck down in a water accident off the coast of Maui, Hawaii. The sabbatical was over, and I had months of rehabilitation ahead. But in this state of great loss, I met God in a fresh light. Because of my paralysis, I became what I call a forced contemplative. Bed ridden and unable to move, all I could do was read my Bible, pray and listen to God. It was in my condition of extreme brokenness that I entered various mystical states in which God revealed himself to me through all of my senses.

One morning I had an especially vivid encounter with God. It was an experience I will never forget. I remember how the early morning sun poked its way into my hospital room and how each ray of light broke forth like a fountain before my eyes. In that instance, I felt the incredible peace of God's presence envelop me as I lay motionless in my bed.

All of a sudden, I was taken back in time and saw my childhood enfold before my eyes. Instantaneously, I felt God with me, holding me by my lame hand, walking me through various facets of my life that I had never seen before. All of the joyous and heart breaking experiences I had encountered from birth up to that point of my life were shown to me. It was as if I was absent from the body and in a different dimension, a heavenly world. God was taking me on a deep journey, revealing his perspective of my life to me. I began to cry with him over sins I had committed and sins that were done against me, but soon an unexplainable joy filled my soul as I saw how much my heavenly Father loved me through each aspect of my life. Soon my weeping turned into tears of joy, as he revealed to me his loving presence that was with me from birth to this very second of my life. I was lost in God, enraptured by his unceasing love that has surrounded me every second of my life.

I don't know how long I was in this supernatural state of mind, but I was brought back to earth when my wife unknowingly interrupted me when she walked into my room. I must have looked strange to her, as she found me in my ecstatic state with tears rolling down my cheeks. Alarmed at seeing her normally unemotional husband crying like a baby, she feared the worst and was about to call for a nurse when I interrupted her, saying repetitively, "Oh, how he loves us. He really, really loves us."

I was lost in experiencing God. The tears I was shedding were not tears of sorrow, but of joy, the result of experiencing the love of God from the depths of my soul. There is no way I can ever fully explain this experience. No words can describe the feelings I encountered. All I can say is that it was a mystical experience with God. Though I had always known that God loved me, now, for the first time in my life, I was enveloped in God's love for me from the depths of my innermost being. God's love for me was no longer just a theological truth; it had now become a pulsating experience. It was as if God was let loose in my soul, filling all of my senses with his wonderful presence. Before, I had read about his love for me; now I was feeling it.

The interesting thing about my mystical experiences with God was that they also filled me with incredible grace and compassion for those who are hurting. I remember feeling a strange oneness with the poor and marginalized in our world. Before my mystical encounters with God, I had always had a heart for the poor and the oppressed. But now, through my new-found mysticism, I felt I was able to enter their pain and feel the anguish of their broken hearts. I also realized that I, in a mystical sense, entered the heart of Jesus. I was actually experiencing a fragment of the feelings he has towards those who suffer. His emotions had become intertwined with mine. Loving the poor, the lonely and those who suffer was no longer an intellectual Christian duty for me to perform; it had become very personal.

In my new-found empathy, I naturally began to encourage everyone I met in the hospital. The sick who shared my room and those who visited with them were important people to me. The nurses who cared for me held personal worth to me. The nurse's assistant who checked on me regularly became a close friend. The abandoned senior citizens I lived with during my secondary phase of recovery at the Roselani Seniors Residence in Maui became precious souls to me. People held incredible worth to me as I was enabled to see them with the eyes of Jesus and feel for them with the compassion of Christ.

I share this description of my encounter with God in order to illustrate four major aspects of mysticism: passionate love for Christ, strong brokenness before God, space of contemplative silence and a deep experience of God beyond reason or intellect.

A PASSIONATE LOVE FOR CHRIST

Mystics have an incredible love for Christ. At the time I was injured, I was finally brought to a place in my life where I was consumed with a love for

Christ. Though I had experienced two previous tragedies, I had developed a deep love for Jesus and was clinging to him with all the strength I had. Everything that had formerly been important to me no longer held much significance compared to my passionate love for Jesus, and I took a sabbatical with one goal in mind—to be with Jesus.

Mystics are passionate for Jesus. Their major purpose in life is to know Christ. The Apostle Paul was a mystic who stated: "I consider everything a loss compared to the surpassing greatness of **knowing Christ** Jesus my Lord, for whose sake I have lost all things. I consider them rubbish that I might gain Christ" (Phil 3:8,10, emphasis added).

Paul travelled thousands of miles throughout the Roman Empire in his quest to save souls. His missionary zeal cost him dearly as he experienced near drowning from shipwrecks, starvation, beatings and imprisonment. He eventually lost his life as a martyr for Jesus Christ. In light of his intense efforts to evangelize the world you would think that the mission statement for his life would be to preach the gospel to as many people as possible, but it wasn't. What consumed Paul was knowing Christ. All the substantial mission activity that came about through his life was the fruit of his life passion to know Jesus. Paul desired to know Jesus in the deepest, most personal way possible. In this, Paul was one of the first Christian mystics.

Mystics are individuals consumed with a love for Jesus. They want nothing more than to know Christ intensely, in the innermost part of their being. As they grow closer to knowing Jesus, they are supernaturally transformed into the very likeness of Christ (2 Cor 3:17-18; 2 Pet 1:3-4; 1 Cor 11:1). When this happens, they naturally become a force for social justice. This is because the Jesus who possesses mystics is a lover of the poor and oppressed. This Jesus, who inhabits the souls of mystics as an outcome of their love for him, is the same Jesus who lovingly touched lepers, befriended prostitutes, encouraged tax collectors, exalted the poor and ate with the sinners. Mystics are filled with Christ and are overflowing with compassion to love the poor and oppressed. The more we become like Christ, the more we will also be drawn to those who are neglected and ignored in our world today. A mystic, in a sense, becomes a "little Jesus" in our world today.

Earlier in this book, I wrote about Mother Teresa's great love for Jesus. As the founder of the Missionaries of Charity, she could arguably be recognized as one of the greatest social activists in the history of humankind. Her whole life was dedicated to serving the poor and oppressed. Not only did she advocate for their rights, she also rolled up her sleeves and worked directly with them. Yet, when asked why she did these things and made so many sacrifices on their behalf, she responded as a mystic:

> We are called to be contemplatives in the heart of the world by: seeking the face of God in everything, everyone, everywhere, all the time, and his hand in every happening; seeing and adoring the presence of Jesus, especially in the lowly appearance of bread, and in the distressing disguise of the poor.[4]

Surprisingly, Mother Teresa's life calling was not to serve the poor. Her divine purpose was to know and love Jesus. She was consumed with knowing Jesus, and her passion for Christ was the force behind her life work on behalf of the poor, sick and dying.

Love for Jesus equals love for the oppressed. A deep love for Jesus Christ must be the starting place for all radical Christians, if we ever hope to follow Christ. But something even greater occurs when we love Christ: "If anyone loves me, he will obey my teaching. **My Father will love him, and he will come to him and make our home with him.** He who does not love me will not obey my teaching" (Jn 14:23-24, emphasis added).

Intimately linked with our love for Christ is the filling of the Spirit of God. Love for Christ opens the door of our hearts for the triune God to come and make his home with us. Jesus' use of the plural (our home) presupposes that the Trinity will inhabit those who love him. And this expression of "making our home" is a perfect description of mysticism—the Godhead wants to relax and enjoy one another with us, like a family enjoys their life together in the warmth of their home.

Mystics cannot help but be powerful social activists because they have God living in them. They have a divine infilling, a power not of their own, that points to the divine entity that inhabits their souls. Mystics demonstrate that our love for Christ is the divine key that opens the doors of our souls to the triune God to enjoy us as his home. When this happens we no longer grow weary in doing good because the triune God does his works of justice through us.

A STRONG BROKENNESS BEFORE GOD

Brokenness is a prerequisite to the infilling of God in our lives. I don't believe it was a coincidence that my mystical encounters with God followed a time of extreme brokenness in my life. After the three terrible losses I endured, there was not one spot of pride left in me. Surprisingly, this was my saving grace. My brokenness humbled me and I saw who I truly was, a spiritual beggar with nothing good inside of me (Jer 17:9). During my trials, my eyes were opened to the many false gods I had in my life, and I realized that though I believed in God before these tragedies occurred, I acted like he didn't exist. I had virtually ignored God for years, taking him for granted as I had placed my trust in me, my ministry, my reputation and my ego over God, his ministry, his reputation and his name. Now, after suffering the deaths of two wonderful people and in a state of physical affliction, I was completely humbled. With nothing left to cling to and no self-reliance, the cry of my broken heart became "God, you are my only hope!" And an immense love for Jesus began to well up inside of me.

It was then that I discovered that God responds to contrite prayers like this. In fact, "God opposes the proud but gives grace to the humble. Humble yourselves, therefore, under God's mighty hand, that he may lift you up in due time" (1 Pet 5:5-6).

Our souls are like wild stallions that must be broken before they can be controlled by the hand of God. Trials are often used by God to break us.[5] Just as flowers can't grow in hardened soil, so it is with our souls. A tilling must first take place in order for us to be softened, so that we may soak in the rains of God's grace, needed to allow us to grow in the very presence of the living God. I discovered that for God to fill us we first must be emptied of everything, good and bad, that competes for his love. God is a jealous God, and in his righteous jealousy he will not share us with anyone else. This is why our walk with God must be based on a love relationship with him alone. And, by living in brokenness, we are in a blessed state of honesty before God that sensitizes us to our tendency to stray away from depending on him. It is a humility that detects the many false gods we might set up before the one true God, and it empowers us to clean house of all false loves that try to co-habit in the temple of our soul.

The great mystic St. John of the Cross taught on the need of brokenness by referring to 1 Samuel 5:1-8:

> After the Philistines had captured the ark of God, they took it from Ebenezer to Ashdod. Then they carried the ark into Dagon's temple and set it beside Dagon. When the people of

Ashdod rose early the next, there was Dagon, fallen on his face on the ground before the ark of the Lord! They took Dagon and put him back in his place. But the following morning when they rose, there was Dagon, fallen on his face on the ground before the ark of the Lord! His head and hands had been broken off and were lying on the threshold; only his body remained....The Lord's hand was heavy upon the people of Ashdod and its vicinity; he brought devastation upon them and afflicted them with tumours. When the men of Ashdod saw what was happening, they said, "The ark of the god of Israel must not stay here with us, because his hand is heavy upon us and upon Dagon our god." So they called together all the rulers of the Philistines and asked them, "What shall we do with the ark of the god of Israel?" They answered, "Have the ark of the god of Israel moved."

John of the Cross saw this story about the contrast between the ark of God and the idol Dagon as a commanding picture of the state of our soul when it is filled with competing loves. He taught the simple reality that two contraries (God and the false god Dagon) cannot coexist in the same space. Just as it is impossible for light and darkness to exist in the same space, a love for God and a love for other things cannot live together. One will overpower the other.

In light of this, John of the Cross was vehement in his teachings about the importance we must have in possessing a burning love for God over and above all other things. Only through our undivided love for God can our soul be the true, unadulterated temple of the living God. This is why he says, "God allows nothing else to dwell together with him."[6] Anything that is placed on equal footing with God will naturally become an idol.[7]

St. John raised a thought-provoking question:

It is the common knowledge of experience that when the will is attached to an object, it esteems that object higher than any other...Since nothing equals God, those who love and are attached to something other than God, or together with Him, offend Him exceedingly. If this is true, what would happen if they loved something more than God?

If you were not impacted by St. John's quote then you need to read it again. His insight sheds light on some very tough things that Jesus said: "Anyone who loves his father or mother more than me is not worthy of me; anyone who loves his son or daughter more than me is not worthy of me" (Mt 10:37).

"If anyone comes to me and does not hate his father and mother, his wife and children, his brothers and sisters—yes, even his own life—he cannot be my disciple" (Lk 14:26).

"No one can serve two masters; for either he will hate the one and love the other, or he will hold to one and despise the other. You cannot serve God or Mammon" (Mt 6:24, NASB).

Let's face it, we are all guilty of idolatry. Often we place "Dagons" of our dreams, passions or pursuits ahead of our love relationship with Christ. This is idolatry, and it is a huge obstacle to the infilling of the divine. I know pastors consumed by their ministries and business people addicted to their jobs. They are all slaves, confined by their corporate masters. Many of us have a deeper devotion to our spouses, children or friends than we do with Christ. Others are immersed in hobbies and sporting activities at the expense of their relationship with God. It is all idolatry, as it enslaves us to an authority other than God. These idolatrous attachments hold us down and prevent us from being all that God intends for us to be. Once again, St. John of the Cross brilliantly shines his wisdom on this:

> The soul that is attached to anything, however much good there may be in it, will not arrive at the liberty of divine union [being filled with God]. For whether it be a strong wire rope or a slender and delicate thread that holds the bird, it matters not, if it really holds it fast; for until the cord be broken, the bird cannot fly.

Only a greater love for God can break any cord that binds us to things over and above God. This is why God commands us to love him with "all your heart and with all your soul and with all your mind and with all your strength" (Mk 12:30). This greater love for God purges us of all the Dagons present in our lives. After all, only empty vessels can be filled and in order for them to be filled with one substance (God) they must be drained of all other contending substances that get in the way.

Mystics, in their great passion for Christ, live a life of brokenness before their God that sensitizes them to anything that will compete for their love of Jesus, and because of this, they have hearts that are filled with Christ. This leads us to the third tenet of mystical spirituality—the discipline of contemplative quietness.

A SPACE OF CONTEMPLATIVE SILENCE

Being confined to a hospital room, unable to do anything I wanted, whenever I wanted, forced me to live a simple life of solitude and contemplation. When I was in the hospital, I embraced each day. As I awoke, the morning sun creeping through my window acted as a spiritual alarm clock, awakening me to the presence of God. In the evenings, after visitation hours had passed, there was an unnatural stillness (or a natural stillness, since we are the ones who disturb the normal, natural silence through our hustle and bustle lifestyles) and quietness in the air. It was during these moments of divine awareness that I was enabled to enter, in the words of the Celtic mystics, the thin space where heaven and earth met. It was during these wonderful times of undisturbed solitude that I was able to still my heart before God and, through contemplation, I would enter through the courtyard of my soul into the holy of holies, where I met God.

Mystics have disciplined themselves in the art of contemplation by carving out space in their schedules for contemplative solitude. They understand the importance of God's words: "Be still and **know** that I am God" (Ps 46:10, emphasis added).

Mystics teach us that it is only in the stillness of our hearts that we can truly come to know God. To be still involves more than taking time off from a busy schedule. We are to slow down our mind and silence the many voices that clamour for our attention, voices that drown out the gentle whisper of God.

In 1 Kings 19:11-13, God tells Elijah to go to a place of solitude so that he can hear the voice of God:

> The LORD said, "Go out and stand on the mountain in the presence of the LORD, for the LORD is about to pass by. Then a great and powerful wind tore the mountains apart and shattered the rocks before the LORD, but the LORD was not in the wind. After the wind there was an earthquake, but the LORD was not in the earthquake. After the earthquake came a fire, but the LORD was not in the fire. And after the fire came a gentle whisper. When Elijah heard it, he pulled his cloak over

his face and went out and stood at the mouth of the cave. Then a voice said to him....

God often speaks in a soft voice. If we want to hear his precious whispers we must first prepare our hearts to listen to him through solitude and contemplation.

Mystics make the effort to hear the voice of the Lord because they believe that Jesus speaks to them. In John 10, Jesus said that we can actually hear his voice. He spoke of the relationship that a shepherd has with his sheep:

> The man who enters by the gate is the shepherd of his sheep. The watchman opens the gate for him and **the sheep listen to his voice**. He calls his own sheep by name and leads them out. When he has brought out all his own, he goes on ahead of them, and **his sheep follow him because they know his voice**...I am the good shepherd; I know my sheep and **my sheep know me**—just as the Father knows me and I know the Father—and I lay down my life for the sheep. (Jn 10:2-4,14-15, emphasis added)

Mystics are like sheep, eagerly waiting to hear the voice of their shepherd to lead them. They know that Jesus loves them so intimately that they wait on him to call them by name. Jesus even said that his relationship with his sheep mirrors the intimacy that Christ has with his Father.

This exciting potential for ultimate contact with God is open to all Christians who are willing to hear the voice of Jesus. For radical Christians this truth must become the ultimate passion of our life. We must desire to hear the voice of Jesus and to allow him to lead us, as our Great Shepherd, in his revolutionary purpose of justice and righteousness. If we intend to do the words of Jesus, we must first purpose to listen to his voice in contemplative solitude. Mystics readily prepare their souls to have "ears to hear,"[8] as they fully anticipate the voice of Jesus speaking to them. After all, "he who belongs to God hears what God says" (Jn 8:47).

A DEEP KNOWLEDGE OF GOD BEYOND REASON OR INTELLECT.

Because mystics listen and hear the voice of Jesus, they possess a deep wisdom and knowledge of God that is far beyond reason or intellect. I remember returning home from my failed sabbatical. On the outside, I was a mess. I could barely walk. I had to concentrate on each movement I made, methodically lumbering along, hands tightly clutching the handles of my walker, one little, weak step at a time. Physically, I was at the weakest state of my life, but spiritually, I had never felt better. I remember the weeks that followed my recovery from paralysis. My close friends had surrounded my family and I with love and practical support to help with our recovery. (My accident had lasting repercussions on my family who had witnessed the event.) These precious moments with friends and family allowed for some wonderful times of discussion about Jesus.

What I found most interesting about these interactions were the comments I received from my friends. They would say things like "You sure have changed. There is a peace about you that I never noticed before." Or "There is a real depth to you that wasn't there before." One friend even told my wife: "Before the accident, UrbanPromise was all about Colin and Judith. Now it is clear that it is all about Jesus."

I remember sitting with some of the biggest and brightest Canadian leaders at a symposium on the future of the church in Canada. When asked to share my thoughts regarding what was discussed, I spoke from my heart. When I was finished the room was silent. The words that poured forth from my soul certainly weren't the regular nonsense that I was accustomed to articulating. Afterwards, the leader of the conference cornered me and said, "There is something different about you. You have a wisdom and perspective that shows me that you know God."

It is hard to share these positive observations people made about me and sound humble at the same time. The truth is that these comments revealed a weak side of me. Before my accident, I didn't display much wisdom, peace or a depth in my walk with God. But after my accident something changed. I was now unconsciously demonstrating a depth to my walk with God that no one had seen before. It is clear that these positive changes were the result of God working in my life and certainly not me. I now had a mystical wisdom.

I sadly admit that there are times that I am still very egotistical, prideful and mean. These are the times I live my life apart from God. However, when I wander too far from God, I have a new sensitivity that drives me to my knees, a feeling that I never had before my accident. Through my mystical encounters with God in Maui, I experienced God like never before, and because of this, I now desire Christ like never before. I don't ever want to return to the old independent way of living I had before my accident. I need God. I want God! And, in humble brokenness, I lovingly and passionately seek Jesus in contemplative solitude, fully expecting to hear his voice, knowing his promises to me:

> You are already clean because of the word I have spoken to you. Remain in me, and I will remain in you. No branch can bear much fruit by itself; it must remain in the vine. Neither can you bear much fruit unless you remain in me. I am the vine; you are the branches. If a man remains in me and I in him, he will bear much fruit; apart from me you can do nothing. (Jn 15:3-5)

Mysticism argues for a wisdom that can only come about through what Catholics call mystical theology, in which we understand God through our hearts instead of being limited to our minds. This mystical theology makes good common sense when you consider that we humans have very limited minds. How can our tiny brains ever fathom the majesty of God? How can we, sinful creatures, ever discern the holy of holies? The greatness of God can never penetrate the limitations of our minds (Job 38-42, Is 40:13-28). This is why mystical theology is needed; it is a grace in which the boundless God reveals himself in our souls, through divine revelation that is far greater than our inadequate minds can ever take in.

SPIRITUAL ACCOUNTABILITY

This mystical theology is not without its critics. Some oppose it, fearing that it can lead to strange heresies and behaviours. It is true that mysticism without proper checks and balances is a recipe for disaster. Thus, it is important to study the scriptures, as they are the final authority over any form of divine revelation. The word of God must be the controlling influence and foundation of a mystic's life. Regular study and encompassing knowledge of the Bible as God's inerrant word is indispensable in keeping us from any form of blasphemous beliefs or actions. But more is required to safeguard us from going down the wrong path.

Spiritual accountability is also a much needed check and balance for mystics. Mystics cannot be a law unto themselves, they need accountability! This is why Jesus said, "For where two or three come together in my name, there am I with them" (Mt 18:20). We need others to guide us in our walk with God. By saying these words, Jesus lays down a strategy of spiritual accountability, whereby we gather together a group of godly people who we respect, who have a deep knowledge of scripture and who demonstrate a life of prayer to be spiritual directors in our lives.

Revolutionary followers of Jesus need to be serious theologians, both in the systematic approach to doctrinal theology as well as the mystical form of theology. We must know our Bibles, and this intellectual knowledge must be balanced by mystical revelation. If we don't have the balance of these two forms of theology, we might very well become a legalistic movement that speaks the truth but lacks the power and love of God. Or, we might posses loving grace without liberating truth. Both extremes are hazardous to Jesus' revolutionary movement. As my friend says, "Grace without truth is like eating ice cream flavoured manure! It tastes real good but is rotten to the core."

MYSTICISM AND SOCIAL JUSTICE

Mysticism is what gives soul to the movement and God's direction to the cause. Mysticism is a fresh wind that must blow through the revolutionary movement of Christ to bring it vitality and godly energy. This truth is seen in how many great Christian social reformers of the past could be classified as mystics. They were known for their strict devotion to prayer and social action, stemming from their foundation of intimate, loving spirituality. Many of them had unexplainable spiritual joy and vigour, the result of their mystical walk with God.

As we conclude this chapter, I would like to share with you a great example of the connection between mysticism and social justice, as exemplified in the life of the great South African social rights activist Desmond Tutu.

In 1986, Tutu became the first black Anglican Archbishop of Cape Town. At the time of his election, the political landscape in South Africa was at a crisis point. South Africa was in turmoil as the result of the horrible apartheid government that continued to rule over a divided, racist nation. The black African majority faced injustice, poverty and physical harm from the powerful minority who had the money, weapons and political might to oppress them. Tensions were at a boiling point; riots and violence were increasing.

But God was at work through a deeply spiritual, contemplative mystic named Desmond Tutu. As the tension and accompanying violence grew, Tutu continued his daily routine of spiritual disciplines. It is said of Tutu:

His alarm was set so that he could begin personal prayers at four A.M. on weekdays. These he said either on his knees or crouched alongside his bed, curled up like a foetus. At five A.M. he took a fast 30-minute walk on the streets…At 5:30, he showered. He was downstairs in his study at six A.M. for devotional reading and work at his desk. At 7:30, he went to the chapel to recite formal Morning Prayer with the clergy who worked at Bishop's Court (the residence of the Archbishop of South Africa). The lay staff joined them for daily Eucharist at eight…At 8:30, he went upstairs for breakfast with Leah (his wife)….Soon after nine, he was back in his office, ready to begin a series of 30-minute appointments from ten o'clock on through the day…He returned to the chapel for 30 minutes of personal prayer at one P.M., then he went upstairs for lunch and an hour-long nap. Appointments began again at three o'clock. At the end of the afternoon, he was back in the chapel for evening prayer with the clergy, followed by personal prayer. He went upstairs at seven P.M. for a drink and supper with Leah and to watch the evening television news. If he had no outside appointments, he was usually in bed by nine or ten and asleep by 11 P.M., after saying the prayers known as compline…In addition to his daily prayers, Tutu fasted until supper on Fridays and observed a "quiet" day every month and a seven-day silent retreat once a year…It soon became apparent to the staff at Bishop's Court that Tutu the ebullient extrovert and Tutu the meditative priest who needed six or seven hours a day in silence were two sides of the same coin. One could not exist without the other: in particular, his extraordinary capacity to communicate with warmth, compassion and humour depended on the regeneration of personal resources, which in turn depended on the iron self-discipline of his prayers.[9]

Desmond Tutu was always on the frontlines of danger because of his incessant opposition to apartheid. Out of the many examples of Tutu's courage, there is one particular event that was witnessed by John Cleary, of the Australian Broadcasting Corporation. It illustrates the incredible bravery exhibited by this godly archbishop, a bravery that could only come from Christ.

It was during an extremely violent time in which young protestors had been killed by the military and police. An angry mob of youth, numbering in the thousands, had gathered together in response to the murder of their friends killed by the South African police. Cleary describes what happened next from the midst of this growing mass of potential violence:

> I heard a noise and looked around and coming down the road was the one thing that you dread when you're in that situation, a convoy of Casspirs, the big armoured vehicles with machine guns on top. You know they're loaded with police and teargas, and you think, "What is going to happen now?" By this time the other bishops had moved out of their cars and were pressing through this crowd of two or three thousand people. I could no longer see them but I heard the archbishop (Tutu) say, "Let us pray." Then the noise of the vehicles stopped. The crowd went quiet. There was no sound from the Casspirs, no sound of teargas canisters. So, I looked around and there, behind me, were the Anglican bishops of Southern Africa— black, white, coloured, old, young—standing between the crowd and the Casspirs, with their arms outstretched. In that moment, I understood a little about what the Christian vision for a new South Africa cost people. I never witnessed that sort of courage before.[10]

Only this kind of courage can come from the Holy Spirit, who dwelt in the heart of the venerable archbishop of Cape Town, South Africa.

Desmond Tutu exhibited the four tenets of mysticism: a passionate love for Christ, a strong brokenness before God, space of contemplative silence and a deep experience of God beyond reason or intellect. He is just one of many mystics who God has used to bring about major social transformations, and their lives demonstrate the strong link between great works of social reform and mystical encounters with Jesus Christ.[11] Tutu also reveals to us the mystic's need to commit to spiritual disciplines. In the next chapter, we will take a look at some of these important spiritual practices that fill us with the mystical presence of Christ so that he works his power through us in a world of evil.

NOTES

[1] Reginald Garrigou-Lagrange, *The Three Ages of the Interior Life* vol. I (Rockford: Tan Books and Publishers, 1947), foreword.

[2] During the fifth crusade between Christian and Muslim armies, Francis boldly met with the Sultan of Egypt in the hope to evangelize him and bring peace to both warring sides. During this time, he told the Muslim leader that God was not on the side of the Christians or Muslims because God takes no sides when it comes to bloodshed. Unable to convince the Sultan, he ended the meeting by honouring him and his men by praying for them. To this day, Muslims worldwide revere St. Francis because of his loving actions.

[3] I wrote a book based on this experience called *The Beautiful Disappointment* (Pickering: Castle Quay Books, 2008).

[4] Mother Teresa, *In the Heart of the World* ed. Beck Benenate (Novato: New World Library, 1995), 33.

[5] I do not intend to imply that God is the author of horrible tragedies. The scriptures teach us that "God cannot be tempted by evil, nor does he tempt anyone" (Jas 1:13). God doesn't scheme up tragedies to hurt humanity, but in his sovereignty, he has given people the freedom to make decisions, good or bad, that can hurt others. God doesn't want babies to die of starvation or for families to be torn apart because of war. He doesn't rejoice at the sight of murder or systemic poverty. God doesn't plan sickness and pain. Even ecological disasters are not part of his plan (Rom 8:18-25). These are all the result of sin, and God's way to fight against these evils is through those who follow Jesus.

[6] John of the Cross, *John of the Cross: Selected Writings* ed. Kieran Kavanaugh (Mahwah: Paulist Press, 1987), 79.

[7] This corresponds with the second commandment: "You shall have no other gods before me" (Ex 20:3).

[8] Throughout the Gospels, Jesus calls to his listeners "if anyone has ears to hear, let him hear" (Mt 11:15; 13:9,43; Mark 4:23; Luke 14:35; Rev 2:7).

[9] John Allen, *Desmond Tutu: Rabble-Rouser for Peace* (Chicago, Lawrence Hill Books, 2006), 274-5.

[10] Ibid., 323-4.

[11] See biographies on Charles Finney, Catherine of Sienna, Teresa of Avilla, St. John of the Cross, Walter Mueller, Thomas Merton and Mother Teresa as examples of some socially transformative mystics.

CHAPTER EIGHT

MYSTICAL PRACTICES: THE DISCIPLINES OF THE REVOLUTION

"Lift your heart up to the Lord, with a gentle stirring of love, desiring him for his own sake and not for his gifts. Centre all your attention and desire on him and let this be the sole concern of your mind and heart. Do all in your power to forget everything else, keeping your thoughts and desires free from involvement with any of God's creatures or their affairs whether in general or in particular...If you strive to fix your love on him forgetting all else, which is the work of contemplation, I am confident that God in his goodness will bring you to a deep experience of himself."[1]

From my years of involvement in working with the poor, I believe that the greatest weakness in today's social justice movement is that it endeavours to enact justice but lacks spiritual depth. It tries to obey God without loving him deeply. It is based on doing good works through human strength, as opposed to fighting injustice by the power of the Spirit of Christ.

Contrarily, mysticism focuses on God, resulting in anointed social action as the fruit of our spiritual devotion. Mysticism goes hand in hand with spiritual disciplines.

I'll never forget the story a friend of mine shared about the importance of prayer in social justice. When he was young and beginning his profession as an urban missionary, he was involved in a youth ministry located in a very dangerous part of the city. Poverty was rampant, and his community lived under a dark cloud of hopelessness. Every night, he would hear the sound of gunfire echo throughout his neighbourhood, followed by the loud sirens of police and emergency vehicles.

One sleepless evening, my friend decided to get a very early start to his day by going to the monastery that doubled as the youth centre where he ran his program. When he arrived, he was surprised to see a few nuns who worked at the soup kitchen on their knees, deep in prayer. For over 45 minutes my friend remained hidden in the shadows of the hallway, just outside the makeshift chapel, enthralled at the nuns praying. Finally, when the last prayer was spoken, the nuns slowly left, ready to go out and be Jesus to those they would serve in the day ahead of them. One nun cleaned up behind the others. My friend approached her and began asking her questions about what he had witnessed. The nun told him that for over 100 years, generations of these nuns had faithfully served the poor and destitute in this very needy urban community. For 100 years, every morning at 5:30 A.M., nuns would begin their day in deep prayer. She then invited him to join them every morning for prayer and worship.

As a Protestant, the kind of spiritual dedication my friend had witnessed in the lives of these nuns was completely foreign to him. His soul was stirred, fascinated by the passion and joy these elderly nuns exhibited in their daily prayer habits. From watching them pray, he knew that the secret to their life of contentment and spiritual power was found in the beauty of their loving prayer life with Jesus Christ. Though his seminary education had taught him many important theological truths, these nuns were teaching him the most important lesson of his life: prayer is the sustenance that we all must feast on in order to make a difference in our sin-stained hearts and darkened world. What these nuns practiced, in their closed cloister, bore fruit in their day-to-day actions, as they joyfully impacted everyone they interacted with.

Like these nuns, we are called to centre our lives on prayerful dependence on Jesus. This is the heartbeat of mysticism that we learned about in the previous chapter. Now in this chapter, we will look at some ancient prayer practices that have been a part of our Christian heritage for centuries. It is important to understand that the spirituality I share with you is not a magic potion to conjure up God but the practices are lifelong disciplines, spiritual graces that God uses to fill us with his presence when practiced on a consistent basis.

When I think of spiritual disciplines, I prefer to see them as sails on a ship. A sailboat cannot operate without the wind. In fact, it is fully dependant on the wind if it is to be able to function at all. It is the same with us. We cannot function as Christians without the wind of the Spirit blowing on our sails. Jesus talks about this in John 3:8: "The wind blows wherever it pleases. You hear its sound, but you cannot tell where it comes from or where it is going. So it is with everyone born of the Spirit."

Spiritual disciplines are the sails of our souls. When we unfurl our sails at full mast, we often catch the wind of the Spirit. This is why we must commit to a regular routine of spiritual practices. It is not every day that we will catch the Spirit. But the exciting thing is this: when we unfold the sails of our souls on a daily basis, the chances of getting caught up in the Spirit are far greater than if we keep them tied shut.

Following are four key spiritual practices that I believe will open our souls to the breath of God.

THE SPIRITUAL DISCIPLINE OF SOLITUDE AND CONTEMPLATION

Jesus was a disciplined contemplative, who cherished undisturbed solitude in order to encounter his Father through prayer: "Very early in the morning, while it was still dark, Jesus got up, left the house and when off to a solitary place, where he prayed" (Mk 1:35).

Throughout the Gospels, we read about Jesus taking time out from his busy schedule of preaching, healing the sick and blessing the poor and the oppressed to spend uninterrupted time with God. The above passage comes right after he had spent much physical and emotional energy performing countless healings and exorcisms. Christ must have been exhausted, but so great was his longing to be with his Father that he got up and left the house at such an early hour in the morning that it was still dark outside.

When his disciples found him, they were very excited and told Jesus that everyone was looking for him back in the village where he had performed so many miracles (Mk 1:36-37). To the disciples, Jesus was a big hit and they knew that their association with him paid off great personal dividends. The time was right to strike, while the iron was hot, as they were bound to receive immense honour and respect from the crowds that awaited Jesus' return. Yet, Jesus was not swayed by popularity. He responded to the disciples' excitement by saying "Let us go somewhere else—to the nearby villages—so I can preach there also. That is why I have come" (Mk 1:38).

Jesus, the mystical contemplative who heard the Father in undisturbed silence, took his cues from God, not man. He acted apart from the temperamental influences of people. He easily left the popularity of the crowds. This story teaches us much about our need for God. Jesus, by enjoying his Father above everything else, is free from the control of others. He does not have to impress anyone or perform for the applause of others. His spirit only cares to delight in his Father. That is freedom!

Yet, how many of us are like the disciples in this story? We cannot hear the voice of God and are not free to do the will of God because our egos are enslaved in pleasing people and gaining recognition from them. When we live for the applause of people instead of the applause of heaven, we become entrapped in a dysfunctional lifestyle of co-dependency on humans to give us the strokes we need to live fulfilled lives. This is a sure way to live a depressing, tiring life. People are not dependable; they will always let us down. To invest our life in people is emotional and spiritual suicide. Only God can set us free.

In his book *The Wisdom of the Desert*, Thomas Merton describes our need for solitude by referencing the fourth century hermits who left the pagan cities to live in the solitude of the desert. These monks left the busyness of the city in desire for salvation from the influences of their society that drowned out the voice of God. Merton states the motivation behind these monks' actions:

> Society was regarded as a shipwreck from which each single individual man had to swim for his life…These were men who believed that to let oneself drift along, passively accepting the tenets and values of what they knew as society was purely and simply a disaster. The fact that the emperor was now Christian and that the world was coming to know the cross as a sign of temporal power only strengthened them in their resolve…The Coptic hermits who left the world as though escaping from a wreck did not merely intend to save themselves. They knew that they were helpless to do any good for others as long as they

floundered about in the wreckage. But once they got a
foothold on solid ground, things were different. Then, they
had not only the power but even the obligation to pull the
whole world to safety after them…We must liberate ourselves,
in our own way, from involvement in a world that is plunging
for disaster.[2]

How do we liberate ourselves from the many outside voices that drown out
the voice of God? Run to the desert where undisturbed contemplative solitude
can be found.

The Bible shows us that God can speak to us in a whisper (1 Kgs 19:12).
This is why we must find our own desert of solitude where silence reigns and
our soul can hear the gentle voice of God. As Henri Nouwen wrote, "Solitude
is the furnace of transformation. Without solitude we remain victims of our
society and continue to be entangled in the illusions of the false self."[3]

MY EXPERIENCE OF SOLITUDE

My time of solitude is each morning while everyone else is sleeping. I creep
down the stairs of my house and enter the desert of a quiet room, where I sit on
a chair and wait on God. It is here, in the golden stillness of the morning, that
I am able to calm my heart and rid myself of all distractions. It is in this blessed
state of seclusion that I empty my mind of any ideas, dreams or desires I might
have. My soul is freed from the entrapments of my personal agenda and able to
be filled with the purposes of God. All the voices in my head are slowly silenced,
forced to exit my mind, until only one voice is left—the gentle whisper of
Christ. This is when I enter the contemplative state in which I encounter God
in a fresh, new light and I am enabled to hear his voice.

The importance of contemplation is seen in John 5:19-20 when Jesus says:

> I tell you the truth, the Son can do nothing by himself: he can
> do only what he sees his Father doing, because whatever the
> Father does the Son also does. For the Father loves the Son and
> shows him all he does.

In this passage, Jesus is revealing to us the secret of his power. He is saying that
he only does what he sees his Father already doing. How does Jesus see what God
is doing? It is through the revelation of God, via the spirit of contemplation that
Jesus is able to observe what the Father is up to so he can join him in doing the

Father's works. This is how Jesus lived his life, and it is an example for us how we must live our lives. Our heavenly Father loves us and is also willing to show us all he does. This happens when, through loving contemplation, we experience God who reveals to us his ways and fills us with his power to accomplish his will.

HOW CONTEMPLATION WORKS

The premise behind contemplation is that our human minds can never comprehend God. As one ancient mystic explains,

> The fundamental point is that our ordinary faculties, sensible and intellectual, are incapable by themselves of representing God to us; that is why their ordinary use must be abandoned. God is above anything we can picture in our imagination or conceive in our mind.[4]

The truth is that God is so great that he cannot help but be a huge mystery.[5] Though we try our best to put God in the small box of our mind, he won't fit.

So, what can we do to experience God? The answer to this question is simple—nothing. And this is where contemplation comes in. Contemplatives humbly acknowledge their need to enter a condition of "nothingness," in which they empty themselves of all thoughts, ideas, requests and worries. In contemplative prayer, our purpose is simply to be alone with God and nothing else. We meet with him, not to get, but to listen and to love. This is why it is so important to deal with any disruptions that can take us away from our loving gaze towards our heavenly Father.

One of the Desert Fathers speaks about this: "Just as it is impossible for a man to see his face in troubled water, so too the soul, unless it is cleansed of alien thoughts, cannot pray to God in contemplation."[6]

It is hard work to be able to get to the place of nothingness where we have emptied ourselves from all the distractions that crowd our souls during our prayer time with God, but don't give up. For the result of contemplative prayer is that you will be able to hear God speak from the depths of your inner being.

This fruit of undisturbed contemplation is seen in another story taken from the wisdom of the Desert Fathers: "A certain brother went to Abbot Moses in Scete, and asked him for a good word. And the elder said to him: 'Go, sit in your cell [hermitage], and your cell will teach you everything.'"[7]

Contemplation is simply spending undisturbed loving time with God. When this happens, we become receptive vessels capable of experiencing God.

MY EXPERIENCE OF CONTEMPLATION

When I meet with God in solitude, I am often led into a state of contemplation in which I desire God to reveal himself to me. I have to admit that often I spend more time in silence than I do actually connecting with God in the depths of my soul. However, there are times in which I experience very powerful encounters with my heavenly Father. When I faithfully unfurl the sails of contemplation in the seas of solitude, eventually the Spirit of God fills these sails and takes me to my Father for a wonderful time of fellowship.

One of the ways that I am able to focus on God in order to enter into contemplation is through a breathing technique that I find very helpful. I start off by relaxing my breathing and envisioning my soul as taking in God with each breath I take, then expelling my own fleshly desires with each breath I release. This breathing visualization helps me focus on Christ as it sweeps away the many thoughts and images that crowd my soul, empowering me to be free to centre on Jesus.

My goal during this time is to empty my soul of all my thoughts, desires and dreams so that it can be filled with God's thoughts, his desires and his dreams. Doing this is not easy, and it is often disturbed by various feelings or concerns that might distract me from God. But when this happens, I quickly acknowledge its presence and then give it to God through a quick prayer of release. By doing this, I see myself fulfilling Paul's words in 2 Corinthians 10:5: "we take captive every thought to make it obedient to Christ."

THE SPIRITUAL DISCIPLINE OF LECTIO DIVINA

Jesus also speaks to us through the Word of God in the ancient form of *lectio divina*, a Latin phrase for divine or holy reading. It is a form of meditative scripture reading that has been practiced in the church, especially among Catholics, from as far back as the 12th century. Lectio divina is a spiritual discipline that involves prayerfully listening to God by slowly reading a passage of scripture and meditating on what is read until a certain word or thought emerges that penetrates the soul of the reader. This word or thought is believed to be from God, impressed upon the reader at the moment it is meditated upon.

Madame Guyon, a French 17th century mystic, described this form of prayer:

> Praying scripture is not judged by how much you read but by the way in which you read. If you read quickly, it will benefit you little. You will be like a bee that merely skims the surface of a flower. Instead, in this new way of reading with prayer, you must become as the bee that penetrates into the depths of the flower. You plunge deeply within to remove its deepest nectar.[8]

I like to view lectio divina as an incredible meal from God. In Matthew 4:4, Jesus describes the word of God as food that nourishes his soul: "It is written: Man does not live on bread alone, but on every word that comes from the mouth of God." When one is hungry one must eat; if not, death will slowly come. It is no different for us as followers of Jesus. We need spiritual food or else we will die.

At this point, I must emphasize the inerrancy of scripture. I have a friend who runs a very successful urban ministry in Canada and recently shared with me her struggle in believing that the Bible was the word of God. She shared her doubts about the miracles of Christ, his divinity, virgin birth and resurrection, alongside other key doctrines of the Christian faith. Wearily, she asked, "Do you sleep well at night? I mean, considering all the sin, despair and pain you witness, are you able to rest?"

"Like a baby," I replied. "I believe every word of the scriptures, and it tells me that God is alive and well and involved in the lives of those I serve. Because I believe in the inerrancy of the Bible, I am able to sleep well at night knowing that the pressure is off of me to solve all the problems facing our neighbourhoods. I believe in an all-loving, all–powerful, sovereign God who is at work in the communities I serve and he loves the people I work with more than I ever could. This is why I sleep well every night. I know that God is in control, not me."

My friend looked at me with a sadness I will never forget and sighed; "I wish I could believe that, I really, really do, but I can't." And tonight she will face another tough sleep.

Denying the inerrancy of scripture creates a domino effect. If you do not believe in the Bible as God's word, how can you believe in biblical doctrine? Without a biblical foundation, doctrine has no legs to stand on and scripture is merely a matter of opinion. If one does not believe in the Bible, one cannot accept the biblical image of a loving God. Sadly, my friend cannot believe in a sovereign God, so she worries and frets over all the problems she feels she must solve since her god is inadequate and weak. What a horrible way to live, what a horrible burden to carry.

If we do not value the Bible as the divine bread of life,[9] we will not hunger for its truth and will die spiritually and physically, like my friend who can't sleep. For us to feast on the word we must first recognize it as God's word. Jesus did. Throughout the gospels, Jesus constantly quotes scripture. However, he does not abuse it, like the teachers of the law did in his day. Instead, Jesus sees the word of God as being food for the soul, not as legalistic rules to judge others by. His great respect and love for the Old Testament supports the reality of the inerrancy of scripture as God's word.

Lectio divina has four stages that are described according to their Latin names. The first step is called *lectio* (selection or reading) in which the participant chooses a small portion of scripture to read, like taking a bite-sized portion of food. The second stage of lectio divina involves *meditatio* (meditation), or chewing, on the small portion of the word that has been selected. The participant slowly reads through the words of the selected scripture and, with an open heart, concentrates on specific words or thoughts that have emerged from the reading, drawing their attention. These words or thoughts become ruminative through repetition in the presence of the Holy Spirit. While slowly mediating on the specific words or thoughts from the reading, the participant enters the third phase of lectio divina, *oratio* (oral), that involves praying or speaking aloud the selection. It can be compared to savouring the food of God. In this stage, the participant brings the word or thoughts to his or her heart and begins to pray them, over and over again, to God.

When this happens the participant enters a prayerful dialogue with God concerning the thoughts that the Holy Spirit has brought to light through the reading. This is a Spirit-inspired revelatory time. Having a notepad nearby to write down thoughts or words is helpful. After this time of prayer, the participant enters the final stage, *contemplatio* (contemplation), in which God's word is digested into the soul of the participant. At this ending stage, the participant basks in the loving presence of God in carefree rest, before his majesty.

MY EXPERIENCES OF LECTIO DIVINA

I usually partake in lectio divina after I have had my time of contemplative silence before God. In doing so, I reverse stage one and four by starting in a state of contemplation instead of ending with contemplation. The reason that I use this order is that I feel the need to listen to God in silence to allow him to dig around in my heart and clean out any false gods or attachments that I have allowed into the temple of my soul. I want to hear God first, without the aid of scripture, so that what I hear in contemplation can be confirmed through my time of lectio divina.

Often, the things I hear God say to me during contemplatio are clearly connected with my time in lectio divina. I always take notes during these times, writing down what I feel God is speaking to me. I then end off this time of contemplation and lectio divina in prayers of supplication in which I bring to God the needs of my family and friends, as well as any personal or ministry request. I always end off with these prayers for two reasons. First of all, I want God to direct my prayers for others. By waiting until I first hear God's voice through contemplative silence and lectio divina, I feel that I am more open to having God pray his requests through me. The second reason is because I have discovered that when I start off my time with God in supplementary prayer, the requests and concerns for others control my mind and become an obstacle for the listening portion of my prayer time.

This is just my personal experience, but the order is a matter of preference. The key is to practice what you find works best for you for it is only by actually praying can one learn prayer.

THE SPIRITUAL DISCIPLINE OF EXAMEN

In the wonderful little book *Sleeping With Bread*, a story is told about the orphans of World War II who had experienced much pain during the war. The fortunate ones who were rescued were placed in refugee camps and received food and proper care, but they could not sleep at night due to the fear of becoming homeless and hungry once again. Nothing brought them peace. Finally, someone came up with the idea to give each child a piece of bread at bedtime. Each night, the children held it close to their chests and were able to sleep, knowing "today I ate and I will eat again tomorrow."[10]

The prayer of *examen* is the bread that allows us to sleep well at night. It is a time at the end of our day to examine what transpired during our waking hours. Examen starts by asking God to bring to our minds everything we thought and did during the day. With a thankful heart, we try to remember all the ways that God used us to bless others and how we also received blessings. Examen allows for us to dig deep into our souls, examining the motivations behind everything we did to see if there were any selfish incentives behind our actions and it alerts us of things we need to repent of that were done apart from God. This process includes confessing sins of omissions, when we had the opportunity to do something virtuous but choose instead to avoid righteous action. Finally, we ask God to forgive us of our sinful thoughts, inclinations and actions.

By finishing our days in these moments of recollection, we are able to sleep well, knowing we have received God's grace and, at the same time, we are better equipped to live for God in a more loving way, having learned through our mistakes. Through the prayer of examen, we open our souls to God's guidance in developing our strengths while sharpening our weaknesses, especially in the way of practical living. In examen, I envision God acting as my life coach, showing me the videotapes of the game of life that I just played, revealing my strengths and weaknesses so that I will be a better person in the upcoming day.

King David practiced this prayer of examen. It is well articulated in a verse worth memorizing: "Search me, O God, and know my heart; test me and know my anxious thoughts. See if there is any offensive way in me, and lead me in the way everlasting" (Ps 139:23-24).

MY EXPERIENCE OF EXAMEN

I often use Psalm 139:23-24 as a form of lectio divina when I end off my day. Lying in my bed I meditate on these words of David and find that they empower my mind to be a theatre in which I am enabled to watch my day unfold according to God's perspective. This allows me the opportunity to worship God, thanking him for the wonderful things he blessed me with that day, and at the same time, I find my heart softened to ask for his forgiveness for the ways I sinned. It is good to end off my day like this—happy for what God has done in my life and receiving the refreshing waters of forgiveness for the wrongs I have committed.

THE SPIRITUAL DISCIPLINE OF THE DIVINE OFFICE (PRACTICING THE PRESENCE OF GOD)

In the midst of our busy lives, it is so very easy to forget God. Work demands, family responsibilities, personal struggles and the surrounding ethos of noise can easily drown out God's voice in our lives. Walking with God through the ups and downs of our daily life is a daunting task, indeed. Yet, it is God's desire for us to experience his presence, every second of each day: "Be joyful always; **pray continually**; give thanks in all circumstances, **for this is God's will for you** in Christ Jesus" (I Thes 5:16-18, emphasis added).

Nicholas Herman desired to be present with God each second of his life. So great was this desire for God that he entered the Discalced Carmelite Priory of Paris as a monk, serving in the kitchen and then, later on in his life, repairing worn out sandals. Cleaning pots or doing leather stitching might not appear to be very glamorous work, but Nicholas discovered that it was during the most mundane of activities that he was able to experience God.

Nicholas' familiarity with God became very apparent to those who met this affable monk. He couldn't help but radiate God in all that he did. In fact, his godly charisma was so great that he became a most sought after spiritual director while remaining as the monastery kitchen helper. The allure of God was so evident in Nicholas that many people asked him to share the spiritual secret behind the glory of God that shone from his life. Some of his wisdom is recorded in a little book of letters he wrote to some of his directees called *The Practice of the Presence of God*. This book is written under his religious name, Brother Lawrence, and it has become a classic of spiritual writing.

Brother Lawrence believed that the highest purpose of our being is to be in constant fellowship with God. He wrote:

> I beg you, what I have recommended to you, which is to think often of God, by day, by night, in all pursuits and duties; even during your recreations. He is always near you and with you; do not leave Him alone. You would think it rude to leave a friend alone who came to visit you. Why abandon God and leave Him alone? Then, do not forget Him! Think of Him often, adore Him continually, live and die with Him; that is the glorious business of a Christian; in a word, it is our calling.[11]

It is not easy to develop the discipline of the practice of experiencing the continual presence of God, but with persistent practice we can try to attain this goal. Brother Lawrence shares his struggles in performing this discipline:

> I began to live as if there were no one in the world but Him and me...I adored Him as often as I could, keeping my mind in his holy presence and recalling it as often as it wandered. I

had no little difficulty in this exercise, but I kept on despite all the difficulties and was not worried or distressed when I was involuntarily distracted. I did this during the day as often as I did it during the formal time specifically set aside for prayer; for at all times, at every hour, at every moment, even in the busiest times of my work, I banished and put away from my mind everything capable of diverting me from the thought of God.[12]

Although Brother Lawrence lived in the 17th century, his words and experiences are a marvellously practical and relevant approach to spirituality that holds much value for us today. His challenge to live each second in the acknowledged presence of God is a sure way of bringing true life to our relationship with God.

One way in which we can incorporate Brother Lawrence's strategy of spirituality is through the divine office, or liturgy of the hours. This spiritual discipline involves setting aside certain prayer times throughout the day to focus on God through special readings from scriptures and the recital of prayers.

In the Old Testament, we encounter this custom. Daniel committed to pray three times a day (Dn 6:10,13). The Psalmist prescribed set times each day in which to focus on God (Ps 5:3; 55:17; 119:62,164). In the New Testament, this custom continued, as exemplified through Cornelius (Acts 10:2,3), Peter (Acts 10:9) and Paul and Silas (Acts 16:25). By establishing prayer times, we can stay connected to God.

I have a friend who sets his watch alarm to specific times of the day. Each time his alarm sounds, he stops what he is doing, pulls out his Bible, reads a Psalm and prays. I will never forget the day when he picked me up from the airport to take me to a cottage where I was going to spend three days in personal retreat. It was a beautiful autumn day, and I couldn't wait to get to my destination to relax and spend some alone time with God. As we sped down the highway towards my cottage retreat, our conversation was interrupted by the beeping of my friend's watch. All of a sudden, he pulled the car off to the side of the highway, excused himself and spent 15 minutes in prayer with God. I was stunned as I watched this man bend his knees and prayerfully read his Bible. His chapel was a grassy knoll near the passenger side of the car, where he prayed, undisturbed by the trucks and cars that sped by him.

My friend exemplifies the truth of what Brother Lawrence taught: "It is not necessary to be always in church to be with God; we can make a private chapel of our heart where we can retire from time to time to commune with Him, peacefully, humbly, lovingly; everyone is capable of these intimate conversations with God."[13]

For Brother Lawrence, being with God was not limited to church buildings or religious ritual. Like my watch alarm praying friend, he knew God is present everywhere and at all times, even in a car on a highway heading south!

THE SPIRITUAL DISCIPLINE OF SPIRITUAL DIRECTION

When we participate in contemplative solitude, lectio divina, the prayer of examen and practicing the presence of God, the Spirit of God will move in our lives. Yet, like St. Francis of Assisi, who misinterpreted God's word to rebuild the church (chapter 7), we, too, can misinterpret what God is saying. We are human and in our weakness we can often justify our selfish desires or blatantly wrong behaviour. Sadly, for some of us, we can even make blithe comments referring to God's will to validate what we are thinking. This is why we need to be willing to not only listen to a group of spiritually sound confidantes, but also to submit to their judgements.

Something wonderful happens when two or more Christians gather together in the name of Jesus. Jesus said, "Where two or three come together in my name, there am I with them" (Mt 18:20).

The phrase *in my name* has the meaning of "under my authority." It was common for servants of kings to give pronouncements or act out requests on behalf of their king in the name of the king. By claiming the king's name, the spokesperson was saying first that he was a loyal representative of the king and has submitted his life over to his sovereign ruler. Second, he was declaring that he was given authority by the king to make decisions and act upon the king's wishes. When we gather together as Christians in Jesus' name, Jesus is present with us in a special way, anointing us with his authority. This is why it is important for us to submit our souls to a group of godly friends. We need authorities in our life to direct us along the right path of God so that we do not get lost on paths that take us away from the Lord.

St. John of the Cross describes the importance of meeting in groups:

> God did not say where there is one alone, there I am; rather,
> He said: where there are at least two. Thus, God announces

that he does not want the soul to believe only by itself the communication it thinks are of divine origin, nor that anyone be assured or confirmed in them without the church or her ministers. For God will not bring clarification and confirmation of the truth to the heart of one who is alone. Such a person would remain weak and cold in regard to the truth.[14]

Gathering together is very important as a safeguard against wrongful beliefs and behaviour. In Hebrews, the Jewish believers are encouraged to continue meeting together: "Let us not give up meeting together, as some are in the habit of doing, but let us encourage one another—and all the more as you see the Day approaching" (10:25).

These Hebraic Christians were under great pressure to mix their previous Judaic religious rules with their new found freedom in Christ. The antidote to this potential danger was to meet together on a frequent basis, so that a time to encourage one another could take place. The word *encourage* can also be translated "exhort." This gathering was a time for instruction in the truth, when these early converts could meet and be challenged in their walk with Jesus. This meeting together as a group acted as a safeguard against any of them going astray morally or doctrinally. It also provided the opportunity for them to receive spiritual direction in helping them see what the Spirit was doing in their lives.

Mystical encounters with God need to be accompanied with accountability systems to moderate what we feel God is saying. This takes place when Christians gather together in the name of Jesus with a willingness to submit to each other. As Paul stated, "Do not put out the Spirit's fire; do not treat prophecies with contempt. Test everything. Hold on to the good. Avoid every kind of evil" (1 Thes 5:19-22).

I am thankful for the friends in my life who I trust enough to submit to. They are wonderful people—godly, wise and knowledgeable of the scriptures. Whenever I have important decisions to make, I ask them for input and most importantly, I carry out what they tell me to do. These are people who have no problem confronting me when they see things in my life that they feel are not of God. I often wonder how many potential train wrecks they have prevented me from incurring by their bold act of love. Whenever I feel that the Spirit of God might be moving in my life through ideas, burdens, visions or dreams, I call on my friends as a sounding board and trust God to reveal to them the truth behind what I am experiencing. By living the Christian life in this manner, I feel a great degree of freedom, knowing that I am in God's hands by placing myself in the trusted arms of my friends.

Your Spouse in Spiritual Direction

For those of you who are married it is important to recognize the vital role your spouse plays in spiritual direction. In most cases, there is no spiritual director better equipped for this role than your spouse.[15] An important aspect of Christian marriage is that the husband and wife build each other up in their walk with God. A couple that is committed to Christ and each other are spiritually endowed with tremendous insight regarding one another. This is the natural outcome of a Christian marriage; after all, it is built on a mystical foundation.

Paul reminded his readers of this: "For this reason a man will leave his father and mother and be united to his wife, and the two shall become one flesh. **This is a profound mystery**—but I am talking about Christ and the church" (Eph 5:31-32, emphasis added). The mysterious component of marriage is that through matrimony, God entwines two separate people so closely together that, in a mystical sense, they become one flesh. The intimacy they share as "bone of my bones and flesh of my flesh" (Gn 2:23) has a spiritual dimension. For this reason, a husband and wife are best equipped to be each other's spiritual director.

I am blessed to have a great spiritual director in my wife. Her love for God and her husband is unequalled by anyone I know. She is intimately aware of all my foibles, strengths, hopes and fears. But most important of all, she is my wife and thus, given divine inspiration to allow us both to walk closer to God and each other. This combination of intangibles brings a spiritual direction component to our relationship that cannot be experienced in any other context. I still need the support and wisdom of my friends, but for me, my wife trumps all of them in detecting the movement of the Holy Spirit in my life.

Final Thoughts

I would like to end this chapter by sharing an experience I had while participating in an extended time of contemplative solitude. While sitting alone in the customary spot where I meet with Jesus, I received what I thought could be a word from the Lord.

In a vision, I saw Jesus weeding in a garden. His face was partially covered by a shroud, but I was able to see his back. With each weed he pulled, he would hold it up toward me as a request for permission to replace the weeds with his beautiful flowers. And with each weed I saw, I replied, "Yes." I could detect a soft smile emanate from his darkened shroud as he continued his gardening, replacing horrid weeds with breathtaking flowers.

This went on for quite awhile. Jesus pulled weeds and, with my permission, replaced them with his wonderful flowers. Eventually I began to realize what was happening. I understood that the garden represented my soul and the weeds that Jesus gently uprooted were the horrible attachments that I had allowed to grow in my soul. The despicable weeds of pride, evil thoughts and sinful desires were choking out God's magnificent flora. Each weed Jesus dug up was presented to me for my observation so that I could repent of it and allow Jesus to replace it with his flowers. I also realized that it is through the act of contemplative solitude that I allow Jesus the opportunity to weed out my soul to receive the infilling of the fruits of the Spirit.

Right after this experience, I spent some time in lectio divina, and the scripture for that day verified my vision, as it spoke of the fruits of the Spirit. With scriptural backing of the vision, I knew that I also needed verification from some close friends. I shared with them my visionary experience, and they also verified its authenticity, since it was not in contrast to biblical teachings. With biblical affirmation and the spiritual direction of my friends, I knew that this vision was from the Lord, and I have cherished it as an encouragement to continue to spend time with Jesus in the garden of my soul.

Followers of Jesus must realize that our calling in life isn't to change the world for Jesus, but to allow Jesus to change our hearts. The soul of Jesus' revolutionary movement is a matter of the soul, our souls. This is the heart of the Jesus movement. True, life-impacting transformation can only come about when one heart altered by the love of Christ touches another heart. When this happens revolutionary change takes place. What suffering people need most are our hearts, filled with the love and power of Christ.

This is why each day I open my life to Jesus by participating in contemplative solitude, lectio divina, the prayer of examen and practicing the presence of God. All of these disciplines are acts of prayer to God to fill me with his presence. I always invite him to abide in me so that whenever I speak to someone, it is Jesus speaking through me. I ask for his indwelling power to work in me physically so that whenever I touch someone, Jesus mysteriously touches that person through me. Whatever I think, see or do, I pray that all my faculties will be enlivened by the Spirit of Christ who dwells in the depths of my heart.

I believe that when this happens, the kingdom of God manifests itself in and through me (and even in spite of me!), impacting my world for the glory of God. I don't want to be just another husband, father, social worker, minister, businessman or community coach, I want to be the living vessel of God, possessed by Jesus. For "apart from Christ, I can do nothing" (Jn 15:5).

NOTES

¹ William Johnston, ed. *The Cloud of Unknowing* (Garden City: Image Books, 1973) 48-49.

² Thomas Merton, *The Wisdom of the Desert* (New York: New Directions Books, 1960), 3, 23.

³ Henri Nouwen, *The Way of the Heart* (New York: Ballantine Books, 1981), 13.

⁴ Johnston, 27.

⁵ The term *mystic* is deeply connected to the word *mystery*. Mystics are people who appreciate and accept the fact that God is a mystery.

⁶ Thomas Merton, ed. *The Wisdom of the Desert* (New York: New Directions Books, 1960), 50-51.

⁷ Ibid., 30.

⁸ Jeanne Guyon, *Experiencing the Depths of Jesus Christ* (Jacksonville: SeedSowers Publishers, 1975), 8.

⁹ The Bible refers to God's words as food (Deut 8:3, Isa 55:2-3, Job 23:12, Ps 119:103, Jer 15:16, I Peter 2:2).

¹⁰ Dennis Linn, Sheila Fabricant Linn and Matthew Linn, *Sleeping With Bread* (Mahwah: Paulist Press, 1995), 1.

¹¹ Brother Lawrence of the Resurrection, *The Practice of the Presence of God*, trans. John J. Delaney (New York: Image Books/Doubleday, 1977), 68.

¹² Ibid., 74.

¹³ Ibid., 52.

¹⁴ John of the Cross, *Selected Writings*, ed. Kieran Kavanaugh (Mahwah: Paulist Press, 1987), 31.

¹⁴ Some marriages present problems for spiritual direction. A Christian marriage prepares the ground for a deep intimate relationship between a husband and wife in which they are enabled to bring divine insight into the other's life. However, this is assuming that both parties are living for Christ. There still is a great responsibility each one of us has in our own personal walk with Jesus. If one spouse is not walking with God then his or her ability to act as a spiritual director is greatly flawed.

CHAPTER NINE

HUMILITY: THE NEEDED MARK OF THE JESUS REVOLUTION

The Little Shepherd

A lone young shepherd lived in pain
Withdrawn from pleasure and contentment,
His thoughts fixed on a shepherd-girl
His heart an open wound of love.
He weeps, but not from the wound of love,
There is no pain in such a wound
However deeply it wounds the heart;
He weeps in knowing he's been forgotten.
That one thought: his shining one
Has forgotten him, is such great pain
That he gives himself up to brutal handling in a foreign land,
His heart an open wound with love.
The shepherd says: I pity the one
Who draws himself back from my love,

And does not seek the joy of my presence,
Though my heart is an open wound with love for him.
After a long time he climbed a tree,
And spread his shining arms,
And hung by them, and died,
His heart an open wound of love.

St. John of the Cross

At this point in the book you might be wondering why so much time has been spent on the interior life of the revolutionary Christian. You might even be asking: Why aren't we studying the social actions of Jesus, the issues of injustice in our world today and how Christians must respond, instead of spending so much time on the inner life?

The answers to these questions are simple. We know what the social issues are. All one has to do is read the newspaper or listen to the news to see the problems all around us. Issues of global poverty, environmental degradation, war and violence, sexual exploitation, child and human slavery, oppressive sexism, greed and apathetic consumerism all top the list. These horrible evils are unacceptable in the eyes of God. The problems are obvious; in fact we have known what they are for years. Identifying them is the easy part. What we haven't dealt with is how our own inner life is intimately connected with our behaviour. This is of utmost importance as injustice and all other social ills are birthed from the heart and made manifest through our actions.

Nathaniel Hawthorne once said, "Eager souls, mystics and revolutionaries, may propose to refashion the world in accordance with their dreams; but evil remains, and so long as it lurks in the secret places of the heart, utopia is only the shadow of a dream." A revolution of justice that eradicates evil must start in us. We desperately need a revolution of the heart.

The strong connection between our hearts and injustice is found in the words of Jesus:

> What comes out of a man is what makes him unclean. For from within, out of men's hearts, come evil thoughts, sexual immorality, theft, murder, adultery, greed, malice, deceit, lewdness, envy, slander, arrogance and folly. All these evils come from

inside and make a man unclean. (Mk 7:20-23)

It sounds as if Jesus is quoting from this morning's newspaper. All of the things he addresses are the problematic issues that are present in our world today. And where does Jesus say these evils come from? They are birthed from within our hearts.

The great Catholic social activist Dorothy Day stated "The greatest challenge of the day is how to bring about a revolution of the heart." The forms of oppression present in our world today are the expression of evil that is rooted within the human heart. It is through the process of spiritual disciplines that we are able to work with God in rooting out the evil weeds that infest our soul and fuel injustice. By opening our souls to the Holy Spirit, we receive divine power to confront the evil within us and to be transformed into socially active mystics. Only then can we be a part of God's solution to the problems in our world today.

Knowledge of world issues is one thing, and there are plenty of good books available that deal with these issues, but to actually act upon them like Jesus is another matter. It is easy to know all about the wrongs in our world, but very hard to take the next step and to do something about them. As James said,

> What good is it, my brothers if a man claims to have faith but
> has no deeds? Can such faith save him? Suppose a brother or
> sister is without clothes and daily food. If one of you says to
> him, "Go, I wish you well; keep warm and well fed," but does
> nothing about his physical needs, what good is it? In the same
> way, faith by itself, if it is not accompanied by action, is dead.
> But someone will say, "You have faith; I have deeds." Show me
> your faith without deeds, and I will show you my faith by what
> I do. (Jas 2:14-18)

Too many Christians are good at speaking against injustice but do not have the soul power to do anything constructive about it. James called this type of Christianity dead. What we need is the inner resolve to deal with our own issues before we can ever target the injustices of our world.

Speaking on the importance of the soul and its relationship with social action, Richard Foster writes,

> We have real difficulty here because everyone thinks of
> changing the world, but where, oh where, are those who think

of changing themselves? People may genuinely want to be good, but seldom are they prepared to do what it takes to produce the inward life of goodness that can form the soul. Personal formation into the likeness of Christ is arduous and lifelong.[1]

To undertake the challenge of addressing the problems inside ourselves is dangerous spirituality. It is excruciatingly hard work to peer into our souls, but it needs to be done. If not, we will end up being obnoxious activists who lack the love and grace of Jesus needed to bring God's peace to a hate-filled world. To be examples of the kingdom of God at work in our world we need to exhibit supernatural grace to all we encounter, both to the oppressed and the oppressor. This can only happen when God rules our hearts.

None of us are immune from inherited pain, psychological scarring, personal weaknesses and downright selfishness. These are the very things that birth all forms of injustice, and they must first be dealt with inside our own souls before we can bring justice to others. Hurting people hurt people. For us to bring about healing to our world we must first receive healing in our hearts. *Let justice start with me* must be the cry of our hearts, and only Jesus can provide the heart surgery we all need in order to be freed from sin and its effects on us.

The surgical tool that performs spiritual heart surgery is the cross of Christ. The passion of Christ balances both the immensity of our depravity, as sin-filled humans and, at the same time, proves our worth through the depth of Jesus' love for us as our Saviour. At the cross, we come to understand that we are stained with the very same sins that fuel injustice and oppression, but we also recognize we are valued and loved by God so much that his Son would die on the cross for our sins.

This truth allows us to humbly stand up for justice as weeping prophets, whose tears are shed for those who suffer as well as those who oppress. By recognizing our own sinfulness and the wounds that the sins of others have had on us, we understand that we represent both parties, the guilty and the innocent. We experience our own suffering in the lives of the oppressed that we serve, but we also become acutely aware of our own sinful guilt in the lives of the oppressors. It is only when we are possessed with the meekness that comes from knowing oneself that we are able to humbly present ourselves to Christ for his forgiveness and receive his power to be a gracious, non-judgemental presence in bringing about righteousness in the lives of both the oppressed and the oppressors.

THE EVILS IN ALL OF US

The truth of our own guilt in the world's atrocities can be seen in the trial of Adolf Eichmann, indicted as a Nazi war criminal in 1961. Many concentration camp survivors testified against Eichmann, but the most dramatic witness during the trial was a Jewish man, Yehiel Dinur, who took the witness stand only to collapse, shouting and sobbing, at the sight of Adolf Eichmann.

A few years after the trial, Mr. Dinur appeared in an extraordinary interview on the popular American television show "60 Minutes," hosted by Mike Wallace. During the interview, Wallace asked Dinur if his reaction to Eichmann was the result of the horrible atrocities he had seen and experienced at the hands of this monstrous killer. Dinur hesitated slightly before responding to Wallace's question and then gave a haunting answer.

When he saw Eichmann, he had realized that he was not the demonic personification of evil that he had expected. It was on the witness stand at Eichmann's trial that Dinur understood a stunning and disturbing truth about humankind: he saw that Eichmann was an ordinary man just like anyone else. Upon realizing this truth, Dinur could not contain his emotions any longer and broke down in the courtroom because, in his own words, "I was afraid about myself. I saw that I am capable to do this…exactly like he."[2]

This incredible statement from Dinur caused Mike Wallace to look into the camera and ask the television audience the most painful of questions: "How was it possible…for a man to act as Eichmann acted?…Was he a monster? A madman? Or was he perhaps something even more terrifying…was he normal?" Yehiel Dinur's shocking conclusion? "Eichmann is in all of us."[3]

Sin exists in every one of us; only Jesus can overcome it. The same hatred that cracked the whips and released the dogs upon civil rights marchers in the Jim Crow southern states of the USA in the 1950s and 60s also resides in my heart. The lack of concern that can cause me to avoid a street person begging for money in my city, is indicative of the same apathy that can be present on Wall Street towards the poor. When I quickly turn the pages of my newspaper to avoid the stories about war, environmental destruction and African famines, I show the same consumerist greed that often fuels these problems. When I sip a cup of steaming non-fair-trade coffee, my self-indulgence allows for child slaves to work on coffee plantations. And when I read about the horrors of genocide in Rwanda or Darfur I am left with the terribly uncomfortable feeling that the people who committed these heinous acts are no different then I.

"Eichmann lives in all of us," and the sooner we realize this, the faster we can run to Jesus and receive forgiveness for our involvement in the world's injustices as well as his divine power to live in the Spirit as opposed to our sinful flesh. This is what Jesus meant when he said,

> Blessed are the poor in spirit, for theirs is the kingdom of heaven. Blessed are those who mourn, for they will be comforted. Blessed are the meek, for they will inherit the earth. Blessed are those who hunger and thirst for righteousness [justice], for they will be filled. Blessed are the merciful, for they will be shown mercy. Blessed are the pure in heart, for they will see God. Blessed are the peacemakers, for they will be called sons of God. Blessed are those who are persecuted because of righteousness [justice], for theirs is the kingdom of heaven. (Mt 5:3-10)

All the people Jesus identifies as blessed are individuals who are very aware of their own human condition before they act out justice. They know who they are and they humbly recognize their personal faults. Their identity reflects the truth of their souls—poor in spirit, mourning, meek, hungry and thirsty for righteousness. They are broken people. Yet, because they recognize their own sinfulness, they are fully enabled by God to effectively live out his gracious justice to both the oppressor and the oppressed. Through Christ they are enabled to be merciful, pure in heart, peacemakers and persecuted for righteousness. This is the way of Christ.

WE ARE PRECIOUS, BEAUTIFUL SINNERS LOVED BY GOD

We are all valuable, precious, beautiful sinners. When we identify our own sinfulness while realizing the great value God bestows upon all persons, the just and the unjust, we will approach people differently. I will never forget an experience I had recently while in my time of contemplative solitude. While praying, I had a profound, sacred moment with God in which I was filled with sorrow and joy all at the same time. Tears were streaming down my face as God brought me to the very depths of my being and showed me all the sin and evil that was present in my heart. My soul appeared to me as a cesspool filled with all kinds of festering rubbish. The hypocrisy of my words and actions came to light that morning, and I wept tears of repentance at what I saw.

However, my tears quickly turned into cries of joy as Christ lovingly removed my guilt and revealed to me the immense value that I have in his eyes. An incredible feeling of peace invaded my soul, and I knew at that moment, even though I was a great sinner, my Father God loved me and longed to cleanse me from all sin.

Then, all of a sudden, I couldn't help but think of people who had personally offended me in my past. Names and faces began to appear in my mind and instead of the normal bitterness I had held towards these individuals, I was filled with compassion. I began to pray for each one of them by name, pleading with God to give them the very same experience he had granted me. I realized that these people, who I once thought were evil and dark individuals, were no different than I was. In this new state of consciousness, I was free to forgive them with an incredible freeing sense of immense empathy for every one of them.

In that moment, I discovered an incredible truth about how we are to approach justice issues. We must understand that those who oppress others are not inferior to us, they are just like us. If we view them as inhumane, we are acting the exact same way that they do towards those whom they mistreat. It is easy for us to recognize the oppressor as sinful, but can we acknowledge that we are as guilty as they are?

We all wear the guilt of sin, but the mindboggling news is this—we still are loved by God and seen by him as being his valuable children. Bishop Tutu acted on this truth when he described the experience of a colleague of his who, while being tortured by the police, said that he "looked up at his torturers and thought to himself, 'these are God's children too, and…they need you to help them recover the humanity they are losing.'"4

If we are to be effective in social justice matters, we cannot forget about the prime importance of the soul, both the condition of our own soul as well as the value of others' souls. Many of us have erroneously believed we can only love oppressive people once they change. However, we need to recognize that no one will change unless they first know that we love them. If people are only treated as evil, they will remain evil. When they are treated as a brother or sister, they cannot help but change. It is much harder to oppress your family or friends.

I AND IT

The great Jewish philosopher Martin Buber describes how this process works in his book *I and Thou*. Buber contends that we interact with others in two ways. The first and most prevalent way in which we interact with one another is through an "I and It" relationship. In this state, we treat the other person not as a valued human being, but as an object or a thing—an "It" that has no value other than what we can get from it. In essence, an I and It relationship is selfish—as it treats others as objects to be used and experienced for personal gain. I and It relationships are formed with the goal of having the object (It) best serve the individual (I) interests.

The I and It way of life is the most common way in which relationships are formed in our society:

> Man travels over the surface of things and experiences them...
> But the world is not presented to man by experiences alone.
> These present him only with a world composed of It and He
> and She and It again...As experience the world belongs to the
> primary word I—It.[5]

Oppression and injustice happen when people are treated as Its. In an I and It paradigm, those who are powerful view the vulnerable as inferior, instead of honouring them as being sacred masterpieces of God. Terms used to describe social distinctions in our society such as upper and lower class, and First and Third World country reek strongly of an I and It pecking order. This allows us to denigrate the value of others and use them as objects to provide cheap goods and services for those of us who have the capacity to mistreat them instead of bless them. Every form of oppression can be linked to the acceptance of the I and It model of thinking.

I AND THOU

In response to the I and It way of thinking, Buber argues that the proper way to relate to people is through an "I and Thou" connectedness. In an I and Thou relationship, we view others as holding a great sacredness. We treat others without any objectification or qualifications. People are accepted with open arms and welcomed by an attitude of hospitality, without any preconceived conditions. I and Thou relationships recognize the value of every person and treat him or her accordingly. Buber claims that when this happens, a divine connection occurs with God—the person becomes the "Sacred Thou."

A story from Tony Campolo, when he was a professor of Sociology at the University of Pennsylvania, describes how Jesus saw others as the Sacred Thou. In the middle of one of his lectures, in a packed out lecture hall on the university campus, Dr. Campolo made a passing remark regarding Jesus and prostitutes. Immediately, one of his students interrupted the lecture by proclaiming that Jesus never saw a prostitute in his life. Tony was incensed at this young man's audacity and he immediately ripped into the pretentious student by quoting scriptures clearly showing Jesus ministering to prostitutes.

At the end of his speech, Tony felt assured that he had won the argument. He felt his reputation was intact and the students would respect him for each word that left his scholarly tongue. Tony smugly smirked at the student, believing that he had proved that Jesus saw not just one but many prostitutes in his day.

However, Tony was left speechless when the student replied, "Dr. Campolo, you see a prostitute in those Bible passages you just read. The people who were with Jesus also saw him with prostitutes, just like you. To you and them, all you see are whores. But do you really think Jesus saw them as prostitutes? When Jesus looked into the eyes of a prostitute, do you really think he saw a prostitute—or did he see a beautiful child of God?"

The student was not only bold, he was right. Tony knew it. Jesus never saw prostitutes; he only saw children of God. Jesus, walking on the streets of our cities today, does not see the bums, winos, hookers, drug addicts or gang bangers that we see. He sees his created children, his brothers and sisters, his lost sheep. He sees God's beauty marks all over each hurting, marginalized or so-called successful person his eyes come into contact with. Love sees things differently!

This I and Thou principle that Jesus lived is present in the life of a simple pastor from Brooklyn, New York. In his book *Our Endangered Values*, Jimmy Carter tells a story of how he partnered with a Cuban-American pastor named Eloy Cruz during a door-to-door witnessing campaign in a poor neighbourhood of Springfield, Massachusetts. This took place shortly before he ran for President of the United States. Jimmy Carter was deeply impacted by this remarkable man, as he had never met anyone with Cruz's capacity to instantly relate to those he met.

In fact, so great was the impact that this man had on people that when he spoke about Jesus complete strangers would often be instantaneously reduced to tears. It was very evident to Carter that this man had a divine presence about him that affected everyone and everything that he came into contact with. When the time had come to end their mission together, Jimmy Carter asked Eloy Cruz what was secret that made him so effective as a Christian witness. Cruz answered,

> "Our Lord cannot do much with a man who is hard." He noted that Christ himself, although the Son of God, was always gentle with those who were poor or weak. He went on to say that he tried to follow a simple rule. "You only need two loves in your life: for God and for the person in front of you at any particular time."[6]

Though Eloy Cruz was likely unaware of Martin Buber's book, he certainly embodied what Buber taught. This humble pastor from Brooklyn treated everyone as a Sacred Thou with utmost respect and honour. Because of this, Cruz was anointed with a spiritual authority; everyone he met was deeply impacted by his holy sincerity.

Like Eloy Cruz, Mother Teresa understood the sacredness of people, especially the poor. A story is told of a newly graduated nun who was assigned to the Missionaries of Charity order that Mother Teresa founded.

Upon arrival, the young nun was welcomed by Mother Teresa and told that she would meet Jesus in her assigned residency at the House For The Dying the following day. That evening, the nun was so excited that she could not sleep. The words "Tomorrow you will have the privilege of meeting Jesus" continuously rang in her ears. After a sleepless night, the nun rose early in the morning and prepared to meet Jesus. She eagerly washed up, put on her habit and had breakfast. Then she met with Mother Teresa before heading off to encounter Jesus. Mother Teresa didn't have much to say to the apprenticing nun that morning. Her only words of instruction were "Today you will serve Jesus in the dying. He is there! Touch Jesus, love Jesus, care for Jesus."

With these words echoing in her mind, the young nun left. That day, she was assigned to an old, dying man who was found in a muddy gutter on the streets of Calcutta. He was full of sores, cuts and bruises. The stench from the little clothes he wore was truly disgusting, and he was covered in vomit from head to toe. The atrocious appearance and repugnant odour that emitted from the dying man did not deter the young nun from serving this repulsive drifter. Remembering Mother Teresa's words, the nun gently cared for her patient. She bathed him, placed bandages on his wounds and sang songs to him. She had no aversion to hugging him while she prayed and recited scriptures to him. Eventually, he died in her loving arms. That evening, the nun returned to her convent where Mother Teresa met her.

Beaming from cheek to cheek, the young nun excitedly told Mother Teresa how she spent the day with Jesus, nursing his wounds, praying and singing songs to him. This nun encountered the Sacred Thou in the dying man by caring for him. In doing this, she experienced what Jesus said in Matthew 25:

> I was hungry and you gave me something to eat, I was thirsty and you gave me something to drink, I was a stranger and you invited me in, I needed clothes and you clothed me, I was sick and you looked after me, I was in prison and you came to visit me...I tell you the truth, whatever you did for one of the least of these brothers of mine, you did for me. (35,36,40)

If you consider the prevalence of wars, unfair trade policies, sweatshops, racism and sexism and the many other forms of oppression present in our world today, it is obvious that every one of them is rooted in an I and It paradigm. When people are viewed as objects to be used, we dehumanize their value. I and It allows us to justify the dropping of bombs on innocent people and call it collateral damage (a military term for I and It). It permits the huge immoral financial bonuses that CEOs receive while they lay off countless workers. But when we encounter people with an I and Thou perspective and understand the immense value they have, it challenges us in how we make our decisions and how we treat and honour others.

The implications of I and It and I and Thou relationships are very important when we consider justice issues. It challenges us to be aware of our selfish tendency to treat people as It objects and opens our souls to relate to others, both the oppressed and oppressors, through a Sacred Thou attitude. When this happens, God becomes involved in our relationships.

THE CHURCH AND "I AND IT" MISSION

Often times we take on justice issues too hastily. I have seen churches burdened with a desire to help the poor in their neighbourhoods or in other countries. These churches raise funds and people to join their missions teams and send them out to serve the poor who live in the targeted project. The problem with this model is that often these churches do more harm than good.

They enter their mission with an I and It perspective, instead of embracing an I and Thou attitude. These well-intentioned people devise a project that they (I) think the people (It) need. These budding missionaries go out and run I and It based service projects from a position of power,[7] hand out clothes and teach Bible lessons, then return from their mission trip disillusioned, feeling that they were taken advantage of by the unappreciative people they came to help.

In reality, these devoted missionaries unknowingly were taking advantage of the poor. They went to give, but hidden behind their benevolence, they wanted something back from those they came to serve. They wanted a spiritual high or to receive a warm fuzzy thank you from a hungry child or a spiritual convert to their religion. Their I and It attitude prevented them from building a sacred relationship with those they came to serve, and by doing this, they inadvertently disrespected the dignity of the people and the sacredness that I and Thou relationships create. When this happens, missions cease to be a holy act of service and unwittingly become a selfish act of seeking psychological and emotional purpose or applause. The poor know this; they can perceive it from a mile away.

This is why James said: "This is pure and undefiled religion in the sight of our God and Father, to visit orphans and widows in their distress, and to keep oneself unstained by the world" (Jas 1:27, NASB).

James informs us about the importance of the sacred I and Thou by stating that instead of just giving handouts to the poor (the widows and orphans of his day), it is better that we get to know them as friends, visiting them, knowing their names and being with them. When this I and Thou relationship happens then God embraces it as pure and undefiled religion![8]

I remember hearing a story of a successful businessman who volunteered one afternoon a week to serve in the local soup kitchen near his office building. Every Wednesday, this businessman would take off his expensive suit jacket, roll up the sleeves of his bleached white dress shirt and slop soup into bowls for forgotten homeless men. As the weeks progressed, the businessman slowly got to know some of the men by name. Over large bowls of soup and crusty rolls of bread, he heard their life stories, saw the faded pictures of their families kept in their coat pockets and laughed loud and long at the jokes they would tell.

One particularly cold and bitter winter afternoon, the businessman left his office building to get the 6:00 P.M. train back home to his beautiful house in the suburbs. As he ran to catch his train, he nearly tripped over a homeless man begging on the street. Glancing back, he realized it was Frank, one of his new friends from the soup kitchen. Frank was in his late 50s, an ex-chartered accountant who used to work just three buildings down from the stately marble office tower where the hurried businessman worked. Life had taken its toll on poor old Frank, and now he was panhandling on the streets just to survive. Frank was just another casualty of a system that often leads people down the pathway of stress and nervous breakdowns.

As the train left the city, the kindly businessman could not help but think of his friend the whole ride home. During supper, all he could talk to his wife and kids about was Frank. When he tried to sleep in his warm bed, he kept waking up, thinking about Frank sleeping in the frigid city streets. Life had now changed for the successful businessman who had a prestigious job, a beautiful house, plenty of food on the table and a very warm bed. He now had a friend who was cold, hungry and in need of a place to stay.

This is what happens when we begin to see people in the I and Thou context. Before the businessman ever met Frank, he saw street people as nuisances who he would throw a quarter at every now and then, just to get them off his back and to appease his conscience. To this successful businessman, street people were just nameless Its, not people. But now, after coming to know Frank personally, the businessman could not help but treat Frank and his other homeless friends as the Sacred Thou. He now had an I and Thou relationship with them. They had value and worth because he knew them by their names and heard their life stories and saw pictures of their families. Frank had left an indelible mark in the soul of the businessman and today, this gentleman spends many hours working with the homeless because he sees every one of them as the Sacred Thou.

CONCLUDING THOUGHTS

This leads us to a final observation regarding Buber's insights into sacred relationships. He says, "Relation is mutual. My thou affects me, as I affect it. We are moulded by our pupils and built up by our works. The 'bad' man lightly touched by the holy primary word ("Thou") becomes one who reveals."9

In other words, those we treat as the Sacred Thou will affect us deeply in a positive way. This also relates to those in whom we might normally view as our enemies. We need to hold those we disagree with in high regard. We must accept them as the Sacred Thou that God can use to teach us divine truth. Everyone has significance, value and worth, even those who to us seem mad. When we treat everyone by embracing an I and Thou relationship something holy occurs: God is present and this means that no one is above reconciliation.

This is how lasting justice and righteousness is birthed. A commitment of humility and love to all we meet must be the basis of all we do. When this foundation is built, there will be a charisma present that will allow people to open up and be willing to change. When people sense that they are truly valued, they cannot help but value others.

NOTES

[1] Richard Foster, "Spiritual Formation Agenda" in *Christianity Today*, Jan 2009, 31.

[2] Charles Colson, *The Body* (Dallas: Word Publishing, 1992), 188.

[3] Ibid., 188.

[4] John Allen, *Desmond Tutu: Rabble-Rouser For Peace* (Chicago: Lawrence Hill Books, 2006), 343.

[5] Martin Buber, *I and Thou* (New York: Scribner, 1958), 21.

[6] Jimmy Carter, *Our Endangered Values* (New York: Simon and Schuster, 2005), 23.

[7] Jesus never operated from a position of power. He was a servant who commanded that we also serve. Christ forsook the I and It paradigm of ministry for an I and Thou lifestyle (Phil 2:5-8).

[8] I do not want to discourage short-term mission trips or other forms of activity that serve the poor. I emphasize the importance of the I and Thou relational component as foundational in all we do. Respectable mission agencies make great partners to volunteer with. In fact, we at UrbanPromise welcome such groups. But we have one condition: any group that comes to work with us must always defer to our frontline workers who have been serving in the community for years. We appreciate what mission groups offer, but the bottom line is that when they leave, our staff person remains. If the group does anything that hurts the I and Thou relationship that our staff have built with the people they serve, it negatively impacts the long-term effectiveness of what the staff are accomplishing.

[9] Buber, 29.

CHAPTER TEN

THE TIME IS NOW FOR A RED LETTER REVOLUTION

"These words I speak to you are not incidental additions to your life, homeowner improvements to your standard of living. They are foundational words to build a life on. If you work these words into your life, you are like a smart carpenter who built his house on solid rock. Rain poured down, the river flooded, a tornado hit—but nothing moved that house. It was fixed to the rock. But if you just use my words in Bible studies and don't work them into your life, you are like a stupid carpenter who built his house on the sandy beach. When the storm rolled in and the waves came up, it collapsed like a house of cards."

Jesus (Mt 7:24-27, *The Message*)

Boom, boom, boom. The pounding bass rumbled thunderously throughout the sweaty auditorium causing a chain reaction of rattling windows that shook in unison with one another to the contagious beat. The music was so loud that I feared the old stained glass window panes, dressed in chipping white paint, wouldn't survive the onslaught from the pulsating thump that echoed throughout the walls of the old church building. The instigators of this infectious groove were four inner-city youth, 12 years old, each identical with that unmistakable urban look—ball cap set to one side, big XXL T shirts, huge baggy blue jeans at least four times their waste size and clean white sneakers.

Boom, boom, boom. The beat echoed on, slicing through the stifling humidity of a typical summer urban heat wave, in an old church building badly in need of air conditioning but having no money to purchase such a luxury. While the sweating crowd bobbed and weaved to the rhythm of the music that blasted through the speakers, the four little performers on stage oozed a coolness that defied the raising mercury trying to burst through the cheap plastic thermometer just outside the doors of the church.

Boom, boom, boom. They danced, they jumped and they rapped in front of an admiring crowd of onlookers joined together inside the boiling cauldron of noise, lights and action. Like master marksmen, they took aim with their words and each one made a direct hit into the bulls eye of our souls.

Boom, boom, boom. The beats played on as these four boys spat out rhymes about life in the hood. The refrain following each stanza of rhythmic poetry made tears slowly drip down my perspiring face.

"We will not bow. We will not bow down. We will not bow, we will not bow down!"

In trance-like boldness they continued to chant these rebellious words, while the crowd joined with them in their refrain of defiance.

"We will not bow. We will not bow down. We will not bow, we will not bow down!"

These words might not mean too much to a stranger unaware of the life circumstances of these boys and those present in their admiring audience that evening. However, for those of us who know these boys and where they come from, it was a holy moment. I watched these aspiring rappers speak out about their lives intersecting with the reality of God as they shared their struggles with temptation and various trials. I was deeply moved by their young voices speaking out strongly regarding where they stand in the face of all the negative pressures they have to deal with on a day-to-day basis.

"We will not bow. We will not bow down. We will not bow, we will not bow down!"

Here were four young boys, living in fatherless urban neighbourhoods, callously written off as festering hot spots for violent drug- and gang-related crime, proclaiming that they will not bow down to the negative influences they encounter on a daily basis. These were children that, only a few years earlier, had their childhood robbed when one of our staff—their mentor—was shot and killed by a gang in their neighbourhood.[1] This is why I choked back my tears. I knew how far they had come and what they had to endure.

Prophets come from strange places, and it was no different for these young radicals, challenging the status quo by their allegiance to a new king and a new rule in their life. Here was the revolution that Jesus began, manifesting itself in the life choices and actions of these inner-city boys, who were standing against consumerism, materialism, racism and anything else that opposed the kingdom of God.

These are children, little kids from the hood. "From the lips of children and infants you have ordained praise" (Ps 8:2).

The Jesus revolution continues and its modern incarnation has some very deep roots.

The rap song the boys performed was based on the biblical story of the three young Jewish captives who refused to bow down to the Babylonian king, Nebuchadnezzar, who had conquered their nation (Dan 3). With wisdom far beyond their age, these young boys understood that like Daniel, Shadrach, Meshach and Abednego, they also live in a world system that tries to force them to bow to the consumerist spirit of our age.

These young radicals were living examples that the oppressed can see oppression more clearly then the oppressors do. These children had what I can only describe as divine revelation birthed from the streets where they live. After all, how many 12-year-old kids can insightfully depict the lies present in our world system as being Babylonian to the core? In fact, how many adults can perceive what these children rapped about?

When I look back over that night I am challenged by the prophetic words of these four children. They have reminded me of how easily I can succumb to the Babylonian structure of our day by ignoring the lordship claims of Christ over my life and the world I live in. These four radicals challenged me regarding who and what I am bowing down to. I want to join them in their chorus,

> "We will not bow. We will not bow down. We will not bow, we
> will not bow down!"

These four mischievous little boys embody the fact that a true movement of God begins with Jesus Christ. They echo the declaration of the early Roman

Christians who boldly declared Jesus is Lord and by doing this, denounced that Caesar is lord.

Over the years, the Caesars have come and gone but the principle remains the same—we must refuse to bow down to the negative powers and influences of the day. These four rebels, in blue jeans and ball caps, have a tough life before them. Submitting to Jesus' reign means sacrifices, challenges and pain, but it results in true life.

RED LETTER CHRISTIANS

Today, there is a movement of Christians who seek to follow in the footsteps of the early church. These modern-day saints call themselves "Red Letter Christians" and, like my four little rappers, they have committed their lives to the counter-cultural teachings of Jesus. By submitting to the teachings of Jesus over and above everything else, Red Letter Christians naturally find themselves in opposition to the current world system.

One of the first times I heard of Red Letter Christians, I was at a three-day gathering of a small group of Christian leaders at a retreat centre just outside Philadelphia. The purpose of this meeting was to discuss the meaning of the gospel and how we, as socially concerned practitioners, could be both biblically sound and relevantly challenging to our world regarding the claims of Jesus Christ.

As we were discussing this topic, Jim Wallis shared his perspective on what he believes defines socially concerned Christians.[2] Jim shared about being interviewed on a country and western radio station in Nashville, Tennessee, where he was asked about the many pressing issues facing America. In response to the questions he faced, Wallis quoted Jesus concerning issues such as poverty and war. His use of the Gospels to respond to the problems of modern-day issues caused quite a stir as the radio listeners had only heard liberal or conservative views. Wallis' presentation of Jesus' teaching on these issues caused the disc jockey to exclaim "So you are one of those Red Letter Christians. You know, the ones who are really into those verses in the New Testament that are in bright red letters!"

Jim took a good hard look at all of us seated around the table and said, "Isn't that what it means to be a Christian? Shouldn't we be the ones who obey the words of Jesus as written in the Gospels? We are to be Red Letter Christians."

This spontaneous statement by a country and western DJ was a revelation for Jim Wallis, and it became a divine challenge to all of us present at the meeting. Little did this secular DJ from Nashville know that his insightful response to Wallis' quoting of Jesus would start a movement of Christians called Red Letter Christians.

A growing group of Christians are using this title to identify themselves as being committed to living out, to the best of their abilities, the teachings of Jesus that are highlighted in red in certain translations of the New Testament. By calling themselves Red Letter Christians, these believers have chosen to follow Jesus over and above all cultural, religious, denominational or political loyalties. They are committed to applying the teachings of Jesus to the most difficult issues of our world and are willing to follow his lead in these areas no matter how much it might cost them.

Because of their loyalty to Jesus, Red Letter Christians are deeply concerned about all life issues, including the right to life, unjustifiable militaristic actions, capital punishment and how we treat people of colour, immigrants and other marginalized people in our world today. They are distressed about the ongoing degradation of our environment and they recognize the call of Jesus on their lives to turn their backs on the consumerist values that dominate our society today, choosing instead to meet the needs of the poor as the primary responsibility for those who follow Jesus.

THE WORLD NEEDS RED LETTER CHRISTIANS

I have decided to no longer tell people that I am a Christian. It's not that I am embarrassed about Jesus, far from it. The truth of the matter is that I am embarrassed by Christians. By telling people that I am a Red Letter Christian I am able to distance myself from the negative portrayal that some Christians have created, so that the focus of my life is on Jesus alone When people hear me say that I am a Red Letter Christian they inevitably ask "What does it mean to be a Red Letter Christian?" and I am able to talk about Jesus, instead of wasting time defending my faith in a debate about Christians.

By calling myself a Red Letter Christian, I now have a foundation to stand upon when I share my faith—the words of Jesus Christ! And I would much rather stand on him as my rock than the reputation of Christian politicians, celebrities, church leaders or supposed Christian spokespersons.

Red Letter Christians wrestle with the radical words of Jesus. We are convicted by Jesus' countercultural challenge to the problems of society. We, like my young rapper friends, have made a commitment to not bow down to the ways of our world. Instead, we endeavour to bow our knees only to Jesus Christ.

Red Letter Christians want to live up to our God-given purposes, and so we must ask these questions:

> How do Jesus' red words impact our world today?
>
> What do Jesus' red words have to do with politics, war, the environment, poverty, injustice and other issues that we currently face?
>
> What is my responsibility in fulfilling Jesus' red words wherever I go?

If we don't wrestle with these questions, we will be guilty of making Jesus and his message of good news look irrelevant to a world that is starving for divine solutions to the problems facing humankind.

If we don't live the red words of Jesus right now, in our lifetime and in our reality, then our Christianity is, as Marx claimed, nothing more then "the sigh of the oppressed creature, the heart of a heartless world, and the soul of soulless conditions. It is the opium of the people."

Jesus wasn't an opium dealer. His message to us was never intended to stupefy us into being people who have our heads in the clouds so we are of no earthly good. He didn't preach a spirituality that separates his followers from the realities and sufferings of the world. His message wasn't just a salvation for individual souls, but he also acted on behalf of the sick, the rejected, the poor and the marginalized. This is the ever-active kingdom rule of Jesus, and it must also be the rule for our lives. To be faithful to Christ, we who claim to be his followers must commit to being Red Letter Christians.

Being a Red Letter Christian is no easy task. It is difficult work trying to apply the red letter words of Jesus to the many complex issues facing our world today, but I am trying my best. After all, isn't this something that true Christians should be all about? I hope you join me on the adventure. It will get messy at times, but I know that our Lord will be pleased in joining and guiding us along the way. "The Counsellor, the Holy Spirit, whom the Father will send in my name, will teach you all things and will remind you of everything I have said to you" (Jn 14:26).

NOTES

[1] I told the story behind the tragic murder of the mentor of these boys in *The Beautiful Disappointment* (Pickering: Castle Quay Books, 2008).

[2] Jim Wallis is a wonderful Christian social activist who has written some very good books on Christianity and politics. I highly recommend his book *Faith Works* (New York: Random House Publishers, 2005).

PART THREE

THE PUBLIC LIFE OF A JESUS REVOLUTIONARY

"If to be feelingly alive to the sufferings of my fellow-creatures is to be a fanatic, I am one of the most incurable fanatics ever permitted to be at large."

William Wilberforce

"I don't preach a social gospel; I preach the gospel period. The gospel of our Lord Jesus Christ is concerned for the whole person. When people were hungry, Jesus didn't say, 'Now is that political or social?' He said, 'I feed you.' Because the good news to a hungry person is bread."

Desmond Tutu

"Before we can pray, 'Lord, Thy Kingdom come,' we must be willing to pray, 'My kingdom go.'"

Alan Redpath

"I don't know how your theology works, but if Jesus has a choice between stained glass windows and feeding starving kids in Haiti, I have a feeling he'd choose the starving kids in Haiti."

Tony Campolo

"While women weep, as they do now, I'll fight; while children go hungry, as they do now, I'll fight; while men go to prison, in and out, in and out, as they do now, I'll fight; while there is a drunkard left, while there is a poor lost girl upon the streets, while there remains one dark soul without the light of God, I'll fight—I'll fight to the very end!"

William Booth (Founder, Salvation Army)

CHAPTER ELEVEN

THE PLACE OF EVANGELISM IN THE RED LETTER REVOLUTION

"Woe to me if I do not preach the gospel."

Paul (1 Cor 9:16)

When I was a child, I played a game called broken telephone. The rules of the game were quite simple. We formed a circle of people. One person was designated to whisper something into the ear of the person to the left; that person whispered the same sentence into the ear of the next person to their left. This would continue and the secret would make its way around the circle and end up back with the person who started the sentence in the first place. Inevitably, the sentence would have completely changed through the process of making its rounds. The lesson is simple: the further something gets from its original source the more likely it will become twisted into something that it was never intended to be. This is why it is important to always go back to the original source.

As Christians, it is very important for us to return to our primary source—the life of Christ as recorded in the Gospels and the examples of his earliest followers as recorded in the New Testament. These documents form the starting point where we can hear Jesus whisper his original purpose for his coming to earth. The words and life of Jesus and the actions of his original followers clearly reveal the revolutionary intent of Jesus and his kingdom.

A DIVIDED GOSPEL

Unfortunately, many Christians do not understand the revolutionary impact of the life and resurrection of Jesus. Like broken telephone, the message of Jesus has become convoluted. Generally speaking, these Christians have chased after a different gospel, resulting in an historic division that has split Christians into two camps.

One camp believes that Jesus came solely to bring about justice. These sincere believers rightly point out that Jesus was a crusader against all forms of injustice and we must join Christ in the battle against oppressive forces. In the past, these Christians were known as proponents of the social gospel, since the emphasis of their gospel was on social action. With their focal point set on societal sin, they tend not to preach on the need that individuals have for a personal relationship with Jesus. People are considered generally good, and any evil that they participate in is simply the result of victimization by outside, sinful power structures. Therefore, individuals do not need to be saved from their own sin, as they are victimized by corporate sin. To adherents of the social gospel, the good news of Jesus Christ is not about personal salvation but corporate deliverance.

They believe that if the structural sin changed, oppressed people will be free to live good and productive lives. To them the issue is not of personal responsibility for evil but corporate involvement in oppression that causes people to make wrong decisions that lead to harmful repercussions.

The social gospel is right in its stance against injustice. Jesus stood against the structural barriers that oppressed the poor, stigmatized the sick and devalued women and children. He rejected the racial animosity that his people held towards Samaritans and Romans. He defied the religious power brokers through intentional exhibits of love and grace toward sinners. He confronted oppressive hypocrisy. All of these bold acts of insubordination against the political systems in his day eventually cost him his life. In this sense, Jesus' gospel was a social gospel.

Unfortunately, this view has led some individuals to embrace extremely liberal positions regarding biblical interpretation to the point of rejecting basic orthodox doctrine such as the inerrancy of scripture and the divinity and salvific powers of Christ.

The other group of Christians believe that individuals are great sinners who will be judged by Jesus because of the reality of sin in their personal lives. The emphasis is not on the presence of corporate sin but the responsibility that individuals must take for their own sinful behaviour. Armed with prophetic scriptures, these Christians believe evil will increasingly abound before Jesus is to return and judge the sins of all people in the world. They feel no need to focus on social justice or environmental issues. I like to call these people proponents of the individual or personal gospel because they argue that the main task of each Christian is to stay pure by separating themselves from the affairs of the world, while at the same time getting as many people saved from their sin before the world is destroyed.

This extreme anti-involvement view regarding social concerns comes up on a regular basis when I teach on justice issues. Usually, there is someone who passionately believes that we shouldn't waste our time with social justice, since Jesus is coming back soon to judge the world. To them, time is of essence, so it is very important to use every resource we have to get people saved before the great judgement. They usually end their argument through a clever illustration in which they depict the earth as the *Titanic*, slowly sinking into oblivion while people rush around rearranging the deck chairs through social action. Since the world is doomed, they want to get as many people in the lifeboat of Jesus before he comes back.

This form of separatist Christianity is popular and fuelled by well-meaning Christians who deeply desire to see people come to the saving knowledge of Jesus Christ. Much money is poured into proclaiming this gospel message.

I'll never forget watching a TV preacher in the US. The man was dynamic, his stage presence superlative, as he stomped around the platform in his black suit, a weathered Bible in one hand, microphone in the other. His voice thundered as he shouted out how things in the world are getting worse and worse—pollution, war, disease, starvation, hopelessness. As he loudly punctuated each problem, the enthusiastic congregation yelled Amen! in favourable response to each of the horrible events he spoke of. I could hardly believe their reaction, but I understood why they responded positively. To them, the increasing evils present in our world meant that Jesus is returning soon.

Our brothers and sisters who extol the individual gospel are right that people are personally guilty of sin. We can't slouch off our evil actions by blaming the system. When the woman was caught in adultery, Jesus protected her from the evil and sexist power structure that demanded her execution but he also told her to take personal responsibility for her actions: "Go now and leave your life of sin" (Jn 8:11).

The Bible tells us Jesus is coming back to judge the world and people will have to account for their behaviour. Only the blood of Christ can cleanse us from our personal sin. Jesus said, "I am the way and the truth and the life. No one comes to the Father except through me" (Jn 14:6). Thus, Jesus' gospel, in part, is an individual gospel.

But Jesus would not say amen or rejoice about the problems facing our world. In Matthew 11:12, Jesus said "The kingdom of heaven has been forcefully advancing, and forceful men lay hold of it."

God's kingdom is advancing, not retreating. Jesus modelled this by healing the sick, exorcising demons, loving the outcasts and empowering the poor and the oppressed. We are not to be people that concede defeat, shrug our shoulders, shake our heads and say amen to what is happening all around us. We are to be followers of Jesus and forcefully advance forward in our world when it comes to the pressing issues facing us today.

Jesus taught that we live in a world getting progressively worse and better at the same time. This dilemma is described in his parable of the weeds and wheat (Mt 13:24-30,36-43). The weeds (representing evil) grow alongside the wheat (representing goodness), side by side, until the Son of Man "will send out his angels, and they will weed out of his kingdom everything that causes sin and all who do evil" (Mt 13:41).

Until that day comes we need to be involved in planting wheat, not rejoicing in weeds.

ONE HOLISTIC GOSPEL

The reality is that the true gospel combines both these views. To Jesus, the gospel wasn't either/or; it was both. Jesus came to save sinners and, at the same time, bring the kingdom of God to earth. Jesus' revolutionary acts of justice did not stop after his resurrection. After coming to earth, dying on the cross for our sins and rising from death, Jesus is not now simply waiting for us to die so we can be with him in heaven. No, the resurrection of Jesus ushered in a new reality: he came forth as a conqueror. The old ways of a sinful life are overpowered by the victory of the resurrection. There is a new order in place—the kingdom of God is here!

This is the kingdom of God that Jesus inaugurated when he healed the sick, loved the poor and embraced the rejected. Now, in the post-resurrection state, the kingdom of God, as seen in the holistic gospel mandate, continues to break forth in greater power through his Red Letter revolutionaries, and it has both an individualistic and corporate impact.

The effects of the social and individualistic gospel uniting was witnessed in the Second Great Awakening that took place in the early 1800s. Countless people came to saving faith in Jesus through the evangelistic preaching and social engagement of Charles Grandison Finney. Finney was a true fire-and-brimstone preacher who challenged people with their need for personal salvation from sin through Christ. However, Finney didn't stop there; he also preached that works was the evidence of true saving faith.

Finney's obstinate vision of the holistic gospel often got him into trouble. For example, in the face of intense pressures from the religious leaders of his day, Finney refused to serve communion to any churchgoer who owned slaves. He rightly believed that true Christians could never support slavery. Finney was also the creator of the "altar call," popularized by Billy Graham and other evangelists, in which people are called to come forward to the altar and accept Jesus as their Saviour. However, Finney utilized his altar call differently. Like a modern evangelist, Finney would call on people to receive Jesus, but he did this before he called them to the altar. When people made their commitment to Christ, he would then demand that they prove their commitment publically by going to the altar to sign up for the abolitionist cause. Those who refused were told that they needed to hear the gospel message again until they truly accepted Jesus Christ as their Saviour, as evidenced by their commitment to abolish the slave trade. For Finney, personal salvation went hand-in-hand with the social gospel.

Charles Finney was a bold Red Letter revolutionary who opposed any form of injustice. So great was his zeal for social justice that it was common practice for him to actually name people from the pulpit during his sermons and prayers in his fight for social reforms. Could you imagine a pastor today preaching a sermon and speaking out against people in his church by name who are involved in unjust practices? He also fought for women's rights by supporting the women's movement for the right to vote and strategically put women in prominent positions wherever he went to preach, allowing them to pray in public during his meetings. At a time when women were expected to stay quiet Finney gave them a powerful voice.

According to Finney, there was one holistic gospel, and his message had a far-reaching impact. Finney's influence on the abolition of slavery greatly empowered the movement. Many other reforms were started by Christians saved under Finney's preaching. Many social action groups, such as the fight against child labour, the women's suffrage movement and the establishment of schools, hospitals, shelters and feeding programs for the poor were all birthed through the influence of Finney's revivals. These born again believers laid down a foundational base for many other great social justice movements alive today—prison reform, inner city work, environmental care and the fight to drop third world debt.

Yes, the whole gospel addresses both individual and corporate sin. It must not stop at personal salvation; it is far too powerful for that. It must also encompass institutional reform. As N.T. Wright states in *Surprised By Hope*:

> The whole point of what Jesus was up to was that he was doing close up, in the present what he was promising long-term in the future. And what he was promising for that future and doing in that present was not saving souls for a disembodied eternity but rescuing people from the corruption and decay of the way the world presently is so they could enjoy, already in the present, that renewal of creation which is God's ultimate purpose—and so they could thus become colleagues and partners in that larger project.[1]

The revolution of Jesus flows through radicals like Charles Finney, William Wilberforce, Martin Luther King Jr., Mother Teresa and many others who have accepted Jesus as their personal Lord and Saviour. They understand the need for both personal and corporate salvation, as they know that Jesus reigns supreme over all earthly powers. Jesus' Red Letter Revolution grows by impacting individuals and unjust social structures.

NOTES

[1] N.T. Wright, *Surprised By Hope* (New York: Harpers Collins Pub., 2008), 192.

CHAPTER TWELVE

THE PRAYER OF THE RED LETTER REVOLUTION

"The kingdom of God has come upon you."

Jesus (Mt 12:28)

If you could go back in time and catch up to Jesus, as he trudged along the dusty streets of the small villages of rural Palestine, you would have heard him speak one main message. If you joined his followers as he strolled on the country hillsides of ancient Israel, you would have seen him live and talk on one basic theme. If you could have been present in the temple courts when he ferociously confronted the religious elite of his day, you would have heard him give one constant challenge. Everywhere Jesus went, he spoke and acted on one consistent subject. What was this important message? "The kingdom of God has come upon you!"[1] To the religious leaders and Roman occupiers, these words of another kingdom were treason! Jesus was stirring up a revolution.

It is clear from the Gospel record that Jesus prioritized the kingdom of God in his thoughts, words and actions. His healings were kingdom of God acts. His compassion resulted from kingdom of God emotions. His acceptance of societal rejects was kingdom of God grace. His confrontation with the self-righteous arose from kingdom of God ethics. His training and equipping of the twelve resulted from kingdom of God expansionary strategy. His death on the cross was the inevitable outcome of kingdom of God love and mercy. And his resurrection from the dead was the continuation of the kingdom of God into our present age!

153

A REVOLUTIONARY PRAYER

Jesus' revolutionary emphasis on the kingdom of God is captured in the prayer he gave his disciples: "Our Father in heaven, hallowed be your name. Your kingdom come, your will be done on earth as it is in heaven" (Mt 6:9, 10). This prayer is a challenge to a revolutionary lifestyle, a way of life that acknowledges sin and injustice and does something about it. Let's examine this prayer and see what we can glean from its radical words.

"Our Father in heaven, hallowed be your name. Your kingdom come, your will be done on earth as it is in heaven." To live a life that hallows God is to humbly recognize our place in this world. I am God's servant and I exist for his glory. Too often we do the opposite. We actually live like God exists to bring *us* honour! How many times do we pray for *our* kingdom to come and *our* will to be done? How often is our prayer life about us, our needs and wants, over and above God's desires? How often do we ask God to satisfy our requirements instead of releasing our will to be surrendered to his kingdom agenda?

An example of how we tend to warp the purpose of prayer is seen in the struggles of a friend of mine who pastors a church that emphasizes prayer. Each week, he urges his congregation to attend the mid-week prayer meeting, and each week he is discouraged by the lack of attendance at the Wednesday night gathering. His desire for a praying congregation and their reticent response to his pleadings has taken an emotional toll. He is frustrated, angry and worn out.

One day, over a coffee, he told me of his frustration: "The congregation really needs to take prayer seriously. I need them to come and show their dedication to God by praying for the things our church needs. We need to meet our budget so we can make the payments on our building, pay utilities and keep it in good condition. We also need prayer so we can grow as a church and if we don't pray we won't get what we need."

I love my friend and truly appreciate his heart for God's work, but I had to tell him that I couldn't agree with his motivation behind prayer. His desire for prayer stemmed from his wants. He was wanting God to hallow him by emphasizing a prayer life focused on getting things from God instead of hallowing God by listening to God so God can get things from him.

The prayer "your kingdom come and your will be done" is about listening to God and then doing what he calls us to do in obedience to God. This is what it means to hallow God's name.

I have another friend who is suffering from an illness and can't understand why God won't cure him. He feels that he deserves to be cured: he has been faithful to his church, tithes regularly, is involved in the music ministry and volunteers in Sunday school. Now he is ill, and God has not cured him. He complained to me, "I have done all these things for God and this is what I get? I have prayed countless times that God would take this illness away and what do I get? Nothing."

The reality is that God owes us nothing, but we owe him everything. Prayer is not a slot machine where we put in enough good works, pull the slot machine arm through a prayer and jackpot! But often we pray with this attitude.

Tony Campolo tells a funny but true story about the selfish motivation that is often hidden behind our prayers. Tony shares of a time when his son was very young and about to go to bed. As he walked up the stairs to his bedroom, he proclaimed, "I am going upstairs to bed. I am going to pray before I fall asleep. Does anyone want anything?"

How many times do we do the same thing in our prayer life? Do we come to God with a list of conditions that we expect him to fulfill and, when our list is not met by God, get upset with him because he hasn't done what we want? The Lord's Prayer teaches us that prayer is not about us but about God. We pray to hallow his name and we seek out his will and his kingdom, not our wants and our kingdom. The Lord's Prayer is a battle cry to leave my comforts and desires aside so I will embrace his desires for the world and my place in his plan. My life must be all about the kingdom of God manifesting itself here on earth as it is in heaven. I can't just pew sit in church, I must lead. I can't flick past the channels on my TV set that show starving children, I must respond. I can't avoid the poor communities in my city by pretending that what happens in these neighbourhoods is not my problem.

The Lord's Prayer forces us to take action. It immediately propels us into a divine revolutionary kingdom movement resulting in a heavenly predicament. We need to be a part of the kingdom of God solution to the problems present in our towns. If we are to do the will of God on earth, we cannot ignore what happens in our own backyards. Injustice, poverty, racism, sexism, gangs, war, violence and all other forms of sin present in our world must concern us.

In the kingdom of God, there is no poverty, no injustice, no war, no environmental problems, no racism. These are not part of God's will. Therefore, being faithful to the Lord's Prayer entails being active in addressing these issues. In other words, the Lord's Prayer calls us to be radicals for the kingdom of God.

As the leader of an urban ministry, I see many forms of injustice that I cannot ignore as a follower of Jesus (and one who prays for God's kingdom to come). One instance stands out to me while working in a low-income community in my city. We had been running a summer camp program for about 90 children out of a convent right in the heart of the community. Every day, the children would walk to our program location happily anticipating a day of music, laughter, crafts, stories and afternoon trips. These children could not afford other camp programs. Many of them came from families who regularly relied on the local food bank. Some were living with their mothers in homeless shelters. Many others were under the auspices of the local child protection agency, as they had experienced various forms of abuse. After the first week of camp, I was summoned into the camp director's office and told that the majority of the children had lice and that some staff members were pressuring her to remove these kids. She asked me for advice. I decided to go home that night and sleep on it before making a decision. I was torn about what to do. Many questions danced in my head. I knew that this was a health issue, yet these were kids who had lice for years. If we were to remove these children from the program we wouldn't have any kids left. Also, isn't this what we are all about— loving those who are hurting?

After much prayer, I went to sleep and the Lord gave me a dream. In the dream he asked me, "I was hungry; did you give me something to eat? I was thirsty; did you give me something to drink? I was sick; did you visit me? I was naked; did you clothe me? I was a stranger; did you take me in? I was in prison; did you visit me? **I had lice; did you let me stay in your camp?**"

When you have a dream like that, you really can't argue with God. I told the camp director of my dream. What could she say? She relayed my dream to her staff, and they gladly welcomed all the kids into their camp. They got lice treatment shampoo and trained the mothers of the infested children on how to treat lice and, to their credit, most of them got lice for Jesus!

This is living out the Lord's Prayer—being involved in achieving his will and establishing his kingdom rule in a very dark neighbourhood, with children who had already faced too many hurts to be rejected further by Christians.

THE LORD'S PRAYER AS A PRACTICAL GRID IN UNDERTAKING ACTION

The Lord's Prayer provides me with a grid to examine my society. To boil down the implications of this prayer into practical action, it means that whenever we see things happening around us, we must ask three simple questions:

Is this something that should happen in the kingdom of God?

Is this the will of God?

Does this further the manifestation of the kingdom of God on earth as it is in heaven?

If all three answers are yes, then I can proceed, whether the cause is Christian or secular. If the answer is no, then I am compelled to make things right.

These three questions impact everything I do, from how I spend my money to what I drive. They cause me to examine the motivations behind my actions, and they transform my relationships and how I treat others. They guide me in making right decisions on how I invest my time and what deserves my energy. These questions direct me in how I react to my surroundings and even how I vote. Asking these questions and wrestling through their meaning keeps me mindful of my role in the coming of God's kingdom on earth. These questions wake me up from living a safe existence—they make me wiser and dangerous. They cause me to act like Jesus, and they have changed my life.

THE LORD'S PRAYER ACTIVE IN THE BUSINESS WORLD

Being a kingdom of God person will transform how business is done. Two of my friends own a successful computer technology company and are very active in supporting various Red Letter causes throughout the world. Their heart desire is for their business to be a kingdom business that makes a difference in the world for Christ.

A few years ago, they were offered a very lucrative contract to work with a dating service in the city of Toronto. The negotiations went well, and there was a substantial amount of money to be made, money that could be used to further the kingdom ministries they so generously support. However, upon further discussions, it was discovered that this dating company had a very unusual mission—they specialize in discreet, extra-marital affairs. They even promote a money back "affair guarantee!" When my friends learned this, they politely informed the dating service that they would have to withdraw their offer due to personal reasons. To my Red Letter Christian friends, this vile dating service did not measure up to the Lord's Prayer. Its rationale for existence (extra-marital affairs) was totally contrary to the Lord's Prayer grid; it should *not* happen in the kingdom of God; it is *not* the will of God; it did *not* further the manifestation of the kingdom of God on earth as it is in heaven.

A few weeks after my friends ended their business relationship with this corrupt dating service, they received a scathing letter. In part, it read:

> It has come to my attention that your management team has chosen not to do business with our firm due to the niche offering our online dating service operates in.
>
> You must be a very busy organization to turn aside new business and new clients...Businesses must wear blinders. How would you feel if someone suddenly chose to judge their business relationship with you based on your heritage?[2] How can you justify the prejudice, hypocrisy and value judgment made by your firm against us or our clients?
>
> Your management has made the most fatal business and personal decision of all—that of a settled point of view.

This letter from the dating service reveals two principles that were modelled by my Red Letter Christian friends. The first principle is that "Businesses must wear blinders." It is true that businesses, as well as individuals, adopt a particular perspective. Red Letter Christians have made up their minds to submit to the red letter teachings of Christ as fulfilled in the Lord's Prayer. In this case, the spurned client chose to ignore the reality of the destructive element of his business because making money is his bottom line. His desire for money has blinded him from what is right. My friends are different. They choose to conduct business by kingdom principles. To my friends, the fulfillment of the Lord's Prayer is their bottom line, no matter if it costs them lucrative contracts.

The second principle of Red Letter Christianity that we see from this letter comes from another insightful comment this deceived business person makes when he wrote that my friends have "made the most fatal business and personal decision of all: that of a settled point of view." My friends did make a fatal personal and business choice. But it happened long before they ever met this potential client. Years earlier, they decided to follow Jesus as their Lord. Because they are Red Letter Christians, Jesus calls the shots in my friends' lives, and every business and life decision they make must first go through Christ. For my friends, Jesus is the CEO of their lives!

The Lord's Prayer has left an impact on another Red Letter Christian friend of mine. Vincent[3] is the CEO of a wireless device technology firm in California with facilities in China and the Dominican Republic. When he opened his facility in China, he was disturbed with the living conditions of his company-supplied dormitories. These small, broken-down apartments contained the barest of necessities and during the summer months became human ovens.

Upon touring these miserable dwellings, Vincent was reduced to tears and asked his management team how they could allow this. Vincent learned from their response that in this part of China human life was not valued, so as a Red Letter Christian, Vincent had to act. He quickly held a meeting with all his workers with the goal to bring healing into their lives by asking them for feedback on how they would like to be treated. Not one staff person responded, fearing they would be fired for speaking their mind. So he asked them to write their thoughts down anonymously on paper. As he read the letters, he noticed something strange. All the letters were in blue except one. It was in red. This red letter described the sufferings that the workers were enduring, and it was the impetus for Vincent to realize his true calling. God was speaking to him in that letter, saying, "Vincent, much is given to you, much is expected from you. Tend to my sheep, and I will take care of your business."

With those words, Vincent immediately began renovations.

During this time, he often travelled to China to know his workers better. By building strong friendships, he was able to create a sacred I and Thou relationship with his staff. In time, he began to make some major changes in their work schedules by giving them weekends off (which is unusual in China) and substantial pay increases. He built a library and games room in their dormitory and trained them to be leaders in their fields. He also intentionally elevated women to prominent positions of authority when he discovered how they were looked down upon by the men in his facility. Vincent's actions led to opportunities for him to share his faith with his staff. Today, a church meets weekly in his facility—a perfect example of the holistic gospel of peace through social action and preaching. And, on the business front, this Chinese facility has earned awards with major US carriers for quality and efficiency.

The Lord's Prayer also has made a difference in the Dominican Republic, where Vincent has another facility that has also got him involved in Red Letter issues. One project he is working on involves many illegal Haitian immigrants who live in a garbage dump in the city of Santo Domingo. I had the privilege of visiting this shantytown, known as La Cañada, to see what my friend was doing there for the kingdom of God.

It was a beautiful, sunny day when I entered this forgotten ghetto. But inside La Cañada, all I saw was hell on earth. What made this even more of a living nightmare is that it is filled with innocent children! Women, children and crying babies with bloated stomachs were all around me, while the stench of putrid garbage filled my nostrils. As I walked along its filthy streets, built on top of rotting, sludge-filled caverns, with raw sewage flowing through this grimy town, I kept asking myself, "Who is responsible for this nightmare? How can anyone allow for people, beautiful children of God, to live in garbage?" Immediately, I began to recite the Lord's Prayer while asking Jesus for his wisdom in allowing me to be able to see what his kingdom would look like, right there in the garbage heap. I wanted to know what his will was for the people living in this place and what my role was in accomplishing his will to be done in La Cañada as it is in heaven. I instinctively asked myself the questions from the Lord's Prayer grid: Is this something that should happen in the kingdom of God? Is this the will of God? Does this further the manifestation of the kingdom of God on earth as it is in heaven?"

The answers were obvious—no. Something had to be done for these people.

My friend Vincent thought so as well. So, with the promise he received from God in China, he decided he must tend to God's sheep in La Cañada. His red letter dream led him to build a community centre to serve more than 3000 Haitian and Dominican families, so they can start the transformation of this "canyon of sewage" to improve their circumstances.

This centre will also eventually house a school, medical clinic and a church. His plan reminds me of the quote that the English missionary C. T. Studd once said: "Some wish to live within the sound of a chapel bell; I wish to run a rescue mission within a yard of hell."

But there is more. Vincent is also planning job training for the people of La Cañada so that his company can hire them and free them from the evil of unjust poverty. Vincent is also using his business status as leverage to influence the political leadership in the country to do more to help the poor. He understands that ultimate transformation for places like La Cañada requires governmental involvement.

I have other friends who, like most of us, are very busy keeping up with family, work and personal demands. One couple I greatly admire run a very profitable technology company, but they find the time to take in sick children from countries like Kosovo so that they can receive the medical help they could never get back home. They feel that as Red Letter Christians they have the obligation to share their home with hurting families who have nothing, so that children can have a better life. Another couple I know claim that they will never retire because if they do, many ministries around the world would suffer from the decrease in funding that comes to them through the tithe that their business provides. Another friend owns apartment buildings in the city where UrbanPromise Toronto operates. One of his contributions to our cause is that he provides free housing to our interns so that they can come and live in Toronto while serving the poor.

These are Red Letter Christians who feel a stewardship responsibility with the resources that God has given to them. They recognize that God has blessed them with financial and material resources for kingdom purposes. They have embraced the challenge to be wise stewards of what God has given them to bless others. As another friend of mine often says, "God has given me the ability to make money so that I can give it away."

Not all of my friends have large financial resources. However, many of them are also using whatever gifts and talents they have for the Red Letter cause. They volunteer in soup kitchens, inner-city after-school tutoring and sports programs, local public schools, shelters and even church planting for prostitutes and street people. They are normal, everyday Christians armed with the conviction that comes from the red letters of Jesus and the Lord's Prayer. In response to their desire to see God's kingdom on earth, they are involved in fulfilling God's vision for our world today.

Like my friends, we all have gifts, talents and influential opportunities that God wants to use for the kingdom of God. So what are we to do about this? As a starting point, pray with me:

> Our Father in heaven, hallowed be your name, **your kingdom come, your will be done on earth as it is in heaven**. Give us today our daily bread. Forgive us our debts, as we also have forgiven our debtors. And lead us not into temptation, but deliver us from the evil one. For yours is the kingdom and the power and the glory forever. Amen. (Mt 6:9-13, emphasis added)

There are many opportunities for us to be involved, but will we take the challenge?

NOTES

[1] Throughout the Gospels we find Jesus relentlessly speaking about the kingdom of God and the kingdom of heaven.

[2] My friends are Asian, so the letter they received was very bigoted.

[3] Name changed to protect his identity.

PART FOUR

JOIN THE REVOLUTION

"If the church is in Christ, she is involved in mission. Her whole existence then has a missionary character. Her conduct as well as her words will convince the unbelievers and put their ignorance and stupidity to silence."

David Bosch

"The chief dangers that confront the coming century will be religion without the Holy Ghost, Christianity without Christ, forgiveness without repentance, salvation without regeneration, politics without God, and heaven without hell."

William Booth

"May this body immolated and this blood sacrificed for mankind nourish us also, that we may give our body and our blood over to suffering and pain, like Christ—not for self, but to give harvests of peace and justice to our people."

Oscar Romero
(uttered during the Eucharist, seconds before his assassination)

"I have a dream that one day every valley shall be exalted, every hill and mountain shall be made low, the rough places will be made straight and the glory of the Lord shall be revealed and all flesh shall see it together."

Martin Luther King Jr.

WE NEED A RED LETTER REVOLUTION

"If anyone would come after me, he must deny himself and take up his cross and follow me. What good will it be for a man if he gains the whole world, yet forfeits his soul."

Jesus (Mt 16:24,26)

The world needs more of God and less of man. This, of course, means that we need more of God and less of religion. To take it a step further, we need more of God and less of the institutional church. Now don't get me wrong—I am not opposed to religion or church. I like the many church buildings I am asked to speak in, and I love the people who attend them.

However, what deeply concerns me is that too often religion or church takes precedence over God and life. Sometimes, we get so caught up in religious structure and the Christian cultural baggage that accompanies it that we have forgotten why we worship in the first place.

It is all about Jesus, and when our religious activities take precedence over him, problems always occur.

This truth became a reality to me and was a motivating factor for the writing of this book when I was invited to speak at a conference on the topic of reconciliation to a group of Catholics and Protestants in one of the most religious Christian nations in the world—Northern Ireland.

From the moment I arrived and got off the plane, I was warmly welcomed by the most hospitable people I have ever met. I was driven around this beautiful nation and impressed by the number of churches that were present on almost every street corner. Nearly every person in this magnificent country proudly proclaimed to be a Christian.

However, there were some glaring inconsistencies. Though Northern Ireland is recognized as a Christian nation, it is also very divided, fearful, angry and discriminatory.[1] These striking contradictions are evidenced by the many neighbourhoods that are divided along partisan lines. Complete swaths of streets and homes in designated communities are set apart for Catholics or Protestants only. In Belfast, they have huge walls separating these communities. These walls are called Peace Walls and have been built (and are still being built) to stop violence occurring from either community. One neighbourhood I saw actually had a gate that they would lock at night to stop people from the other side of the wall from coming into their neighbourhood to cause trouble. Though the violent acts of shootings and bombings have slowed down recently, there still are threats, beatings and the occasional killing. Even with the limited manifestations of violence, religious segregation still exists between Catholics and Protestants, and all of this is happening in a Christian nation filled with Christian churches!

My first session with my Catholic and Protestant brothers and sisters didn't go very well. I felt that my words were bouncing off a wall of unseen division and complacency between my listeners. So, after my session was over, I went back to the room where I was staying and feverishly spent the rest of the day working on a new lecture to be presented for the second session that was to take place the next morning. As I started to write my outline, I prayed for the wonderful people of Northern Ireland, beseeching God for the right message to give them. After I prayed, I quieted my soul to hear God.

All I could think of was Jesus. Give them Jesus. Teach about Jesus. Preach on the red letters of Jesus. So, this is what I did. I spoke on how religion does not unite but divides. I stated that Catholics and Protestants can never agree on their religious rituals and beliefs. I even told my Protestant brethren that they cannot even agree with each other, as they were all divided according to their denominational backgrounds. This was all wrong because Jesus came to bring unity (Jn 17:20-21).

I shared Matthew 9:16-17, where Jesus taught how his revolution would bring about a new wine (Jesus' gospel) that can only be held in a new wineskin (Jesus' revolutionary movement). Explaining to my listeners that it was time for them to abandon the old wineskin of their religious customs, I encouraged them to embrace the new wineskin of Jesus' revolutionary movement—the Red Letter movement. To me, it was clear that their religion wasn't working and hadn't worked for centuries. I challenged them to surrender their religious paradigms and embrace the one true thing we could all agree on—Jesus Christ!

Then I asked them to do something radical. Since Jesus is the only thing that both Catholics and Protestants could be united about, why not do it? Why not gather together weekly, in small groups, Catholic and Protestant together, to worship and pray to Christ, read his Gospels and listen to his voice for what he wanted them to do in Northern Ireland? Yes, it was alright for them to still go to mass or Sunday service, but the challenge was for them to meet together on another day of the week to hear Jesus.

Today, there are a few Red Letter Christians meeting together to enact Jesus' dreams for Northern Ireland. One of these revolutionaries is a young man named Garret,[2] who was assigned to be my driver and host when I was speaking there. One evening, as we sat in an old Irish pub, Garret told me a fascinating story of how a local Catholic church building was vandalized by some young Protestant toughs. Angry youths had spray-painted incendiary words and pictures along the front wall of the church. In response, Garret took a group of Protestant young people and visited with the priest of the church, apologizing in the name of Jesus for what had been done. Then, they went right to work, scrubbing the walls clean of the repulsive graffiti.

This practical act of love from a group of Red Letter Christians attracted the attention of the media, who covered the story in the newspaper. It also caught the eye of the local Protestant paramilitary that ruled the streets in this town. Garret was quickly summoned to meet with the leader of this illegal gang. With fear and trembling, Garret walked into a darkened pub, where he was ushered in by two men to where their leader sat. There, seated in a corner of the pub, face staring out at Garret, was a huge man. A chair was shoved in Garret's direction, and he sat down. Then, he was asked by the man "Why did you do that? Why did you clean up that Catholic church?" Garret replied, "Because I am a Christian and this is what Jesus wanted me to do." This response caught the paramilitary leader off guard. He stared at Garret, looking him up and down for what seemed like an eternity, and then said, "Okay, that is a good answer. Tell me more about this Jesus." Garret ended up meeting with this man countless times, and even had him meet with the Catholic priest, as well as the local Catholic paramilitary. One day, I received an astonishing e-mail from my good friend Garret. It said:

> Just want to keep you up to date with things here. I'm not sure you remember the paramilitary guy I mentioned when I was doing mediation between him and the Catholic church. Well, I just heard he gave his life to Jesus last week. How amazing is that???

Imagine what would happen to Northern Ireland if we had more Red Letter Christians like Garret in that wonderful nation? Imagine if small groups of Catholics and Protestants throughout Northern Ireland banded together and did these types of revolutionary Red Letter Movement actions? After all, Jesus desires that we be unified (Jn 17:20-21) and that those who seek to follow him set their differences aside to meet as one for the sake of Christ. If more Catholics and Protestants in Northern Ireland did this, what a great impression they would make on the rest of the divided country. What great things Jesus would call them to as they gather together to fulfill his red letters and the Lord's Prayer in Northern Ireland today!

When I think about the challenge that was given to the Irish, I can't help but dream about our world. Red Letter Christianity is God's dream for every nation in our world, not just Ireland. What would happen if Christians every-where joined together as Red Letter Christians committed to act out the words of Jesus and to fulfill the Lord's Prayer locally, nationally and globally? What would be the impact of Red Letter groups, spread out throughout the world, worshipping Christ, listening to his voice and doing his works? Imagine the impact that these groups would have in their cities, nation and world!

NO LONE RANGERS IN THE RED LETTER MOVEMENT

It is very important that we understand that the Red Letter Revolution can only take place within community. Just as we can't rely on our own strength, but need the power of the Holy Spirit, we cannot live a revolutionary life in isola-tion. For us to live out the radical ways of Jesus, it is imperative for us to join a community of like-minded revolutionaries to help us in following Jesus.

The importance of community cannot be understated. Howard Snyder writes: "The challenge before us today is to be radically committed to Jesus and his reign and, precisely for that reason, to be radically committed to the world God has made. This is possible in only one way: through radical commitment to one another in the body of Christ."[3]

Jesus never intended his movement to be filled with lone rangers. This is why he modelled community by calling people to join him in his revolutionary mission. When Jesus healed the sick, cast out demons, confronted his adversaries and preached the good news, he was almost always with his disciples.

When he sent out the twelve disciples, he sent them in small groups, never alone (Mk 6:7, Lk 9:1-2). When he taught the disciples to pray, he did so in a plural form, instructing them to address God as *our* father and to ask their heavenly father to give *us*, forgive *us*, lead *us*, deliver *us* (Mt 6:9-13; Lk 11:2-4). He even encouraged them to gather in groups: "Where two or three come together in my name, there am I with them" (Mt 18:20). These followers of Jesus obeyed his call to gather together by meeting in house churches and doing ministry in teams.[4] This aspect of communal Christian faith is also reflected in that most of the New Testament books are addressed to communities of believers, not just individuals.

These early revolutionaries understood the need for communal encouragement in the face of fundamental opposition. This is because Jesus and his early followers knew that to live as a Red Letter Christian is no easy task. To be involved in a subversive, countercultural movement is a necessary but dangerous struggle; in order to be successful in fulfilling the revolution, help was needed.

COMMUNITAS

When I think of the importance of community in fulfilling Jesus' Red Letter Revolution, I am reminded of the teachings of anthropologist Victor Turner.[5] Turner observed the power of community while studying the rites of passage of boys from African tribal societies. He shares stories of how these boys were kept under the care of their mothers until initiation age.

Then, each year, at the appropriate time, the men of the village would sneak into the female compound and kidnap the boys who were of age. These boys were blindfolded, roughed up and herded out together into the jungle, where they are circumcised and left to fend for themselves for a period of about six months. Once a month, the elders of the village would enter the jungle to meet with the boys and mentor them, but outside of these monthly meetings, the boys were left alone to fend for themselves.

In the beginning stages of this initiation, the boys always tried to survive on their own, but they would soon realize that their chances of survival were far greater by bonding together. This formation of community that occurred between these boys was based on one purpose—survival. In time, the sense of belonging and social togetherness brought about by their need to rely on each other became so intimate and meaningful that Turner could not use the word *community*, or any other word, to describe what was happening with these boys. So, he created a new word to describe the incredible camaraderie experienced when a group gathers together in dependence on each other for survival: *communitas*.

Turner's description of real community is a perfect illustration of what the early church possessed. The early Christians possessed a depth of fellowship that was forged in the fires of persecution. They experienced communitas by sharing their meals, finances, food, homes and other things with one another as they worked together as revolutionaries of Jesus.

It should be the same for us today. Red Letter Christians need communitas. It is imperative to meet regularly as a group of like-minded revolutionaries. We must have constant encouragement, instruction, evaluation and accountability to continue in the radical ways of Jesus, so that we do not give up on the revolution by surrendering our values to a corrupt, selfish, materialistic realm. We need to see ourselves as those African boys, thrown into the jungle of the world to face many dangers we cannot fight alone. The danger is imminent, communitas is needed.

Communitas is the result of a joined commitment to fulfill the Red Letter Revolution of Jesus. Jean Vanier, founder of L'Arche communities, describes Christian communities:

> It is when the members of a community realize that they are not there simply for themselves or their own sanctification, but to welcome the gift of God, to hasten his kingdom and to quench the thirst in parched hearts through their prayer and sacrifice, love and acts of service, that they will truly live community. A community is called to be a light in a world of darkness, a spring of fresh water in the church and for all people.[6]

True Red Letter Christian communities are not Christian self-help groups. Nor are they Bible study groups that exist to satisfy theological curiosities. No, true Christian community, real communitas, can only come about when we base our gathering together on loving God and extending his love to a hurting world through mission.

At UrbanPromise Toronto, we make it a non-negotiable that our staff members gather together weekly for prayer and worship. The reason for this is that we experience long, gruelling days in the trenches serving Jesus by encountering some very heavy ministry ordeals. As I often tell my staff, "You are all sponges that soak up the pain and sin of those you serve. This is a good thing, as the people you serve need you in their lives. They need you to soak up their pain for their burdens are far too heavy for them to carry alone. However, sponges that are not rinsed will eventually leak. You can only carry others burdens for so long." So, where do we rinse out our sponges? At the cross of Christ when we meet together weekly as a staff.

Communitas is experienced at these weekly staff gatherings because Jesus presents himself to us through those gathered together, as we depend on each other, exhort each other and heal each other while we serve together in Jesus' revolutionary mission. When we meet together, we discover the truth that Jesus Christ is the ultimate sponge that takes away the sins of the world, and every week, we have the privilege to empty ourselves of all the pain and sin we have taken on by serving many hurting people.

This kind of Christian communitas is not only for those who are recognized as full-time missionaries. The truth be told, we are all full-time missionaries. All of us are to be Red Letter revolutionaries wherever God has placed us. Now imagine with me what could happen if groups of Red Letter Christians, from all aspects of life, met together on a weekly basis to hear from Jesus, do mission and empty their sponges? Picture five or ten people gathering together regularly, with mission in mind? In this group are business people, housewives, teenagers and retired individuals, all committed to act on the red letters of Jesus and the Lord's Prayer in using their sphere of influence to impact their world through the power of Jesus. Is this not true Christianity?

Jesus has called us to a revolutionary purpose and has provided us the power to fulfill his revolution through the Holy Spirit, but it is a completely different matter to actually *do* what we have learned. If we want to be Red Letter Christians who are known for our actions of justice on behalf of the poor and oppressed, then we must act on the words of the great revolutionary James, who said, "Do not merely listen to [or read] the word, and so deceive yourselves. Do what it says" (1:22). In light of James words, let us pursue the life of a Red Letter Christian.

JOIN THE RED LETTER REVOLUTION

The life and words of Jesus call us to live a revolutionary life. My prayer is that you will join a movement of individuals who are reading and then acting upon the message of Jesus Christ.

You can join this Red Letter Christian movement by applying the principles in this book to your life. First, we must all realize that Jesus was a revolutionary. Don't settle for the domesticated version of a safe, conservative, religious Christianity that is far too prevalent in the Western world today. The revolutionary acts of Christ provide us with a radical framework in which we can realize the revolutionary agenda of Jesus and join him in standing up against any religious or political power that chooses to ignore the poor and oppressed. The first step to becoming a Red Letter Christian is to realize that Jesus is calling us to be his revolutionaries in a world of despair.

Secondly, we need to engage ourselves in the spiritual practices that Jesus exemplified. To be part of the Jesus revolution, Red Letter Christians must practice the spiritual disciplines of encountering God through the prayerful surrender of our souls so that we will become mystical activists who love God in all we do. It is only by having the fullness of Jesus dwelling inside of us that we can accomplish his revolutionary actions, especially on behalf of the poor and oppressed. Engaging in the Spirit through spiritual disciplines is the second step to becoming a Red Letter Christian.

Finally, to be a Red Letter Christian, we must do the works of Jesus in our world today. We must look to the public life of Jesus for how to live. Once we realize the radical implications of the Jesus revolution and engage in spiritual practices that fill us with the power of the Holy Spirit, we must commit to do what Jesus tells us to in our world of evil, sin and injustice. To help, we can ask the simple, clear questions of the red letters of Jesus and use the Lord's Prayer to guide us on the revolutionary path of Jesus.

Realizing the revolutionary life of Jesus, engaging in the spiritual practices of Jesus and doing the works of Jesus is what the Red Letter Revolution is all about.

WILL YOU JOIN THE RED LETTER REVOLUTION?

Jesus is the answer! Not church, not religion but Jesus. He is the divine solution we desperately need to address our human problems. And his challenge could not be more clear and simple: join Jesus' new wineskin and embrace the new wine of Jesus' revolutionary gospel—the Red Letter Movement. There is no other way, no other option. Jesus allows no escape clause. We must either be for him or be against him. "This is war, and there is no neutral ground. If you're not on my side, you're the enemy; if you're not helping, you're making things worse" (Mt 12:30, *The Message*).

So, what will it be? Will you join Jesus' Red Letter Revolution or will you remain on the sidelines? The choice is yours and many await your fateful decision. One of the persons God wants to touch through you is a young child named Kadeem.

Kadeem is a 10-year-old boy who is part of our program at UrbanPromise Toronto. He lives in a government housing project that has a reputation for drugs, gangs and violence. One day, after a particularly bloody weekend of drug inspired violence, my staff found Kadeem crying as they walked him home from our after-school program he faithfully attends every day. With great big tears running down his cheeks, Kadeem blurted out, "I am sick and tired of all the guns and knives in my neighbourhood." One of my staff realized that Kadeem might be suffering from urban post-traumatic syndrome and took him aside to spend some time with him. They talked for a few minutes and then my staff person asked Kadeem, "What can you do about all the guns and knives?" Kadeem stared down at the ground beneath him, as if the answer to this question was somehow hidden in the concrete below his feet. Then, he straightened up and replied, "One day I am going to be the president of the world and get rid of every gun and knife that is out there." "What else can you do Kadeem?" asked my staff person. And Kadeem replied, "I can pray to God that he will keep us all safe." And every night, in my city, a little child prays that God will rid the world of guns and knives.

When I think of Kadeem, I am reminded of Jesus weeping over the city.

> How often I have longed to gather your children together, as a hen gathers her chicks under her wings, but you were not willing. Look, your house is left to you desolate. For I tell you, you will not see me again until you say, "Blessed is he who comes in the name of the Lord." (Mt 23:37-39, *The Message*)

What will bring healing to Kadeem's neighbourhood? What will bring peace to his city? Who can transform a violent world of poverty and oppression? Listen to Jesus: "Blessed is he who comes in the name of the Lord." Red Letter Christians are the ones who come in the name of Jesus. Will you join the revolution?

NOTES

[1] To my dear readers of Irish ancestry who might be upset with what they are reading: I humbly admit that I am Irish. My parents were both born and raised in Belfast, and many of my family still live there. Most of my ancestors belonged to the Orange Order, including my great grandfather and political activist, Arthur Trew, who was the recipient of various death threats as the result of his inflammatory, anti-Catholic oratory. Many a good Irish riot took place as the result of his speeches.

[2] Name changed to protect his identity.

[3] Howard Snyder, *A Kingdom Manifesto* (Downers Grove: InterVarsity Press, 1985), 82.

[4] The Book of Acts records Paul's mission trips as team work with Barnabas, Silas and Timothy.

[5] Hirsch, 220.

[6] Jean Vanier, *Community and Growth* (Mahwah, New Jersey: Paulist Press, 1989), 89.

DIAGRAM OF RED LETTER CHRISTIANITY

THE RED LETTER MOVEMENT

"If anyone would come after me, he must deny himself and take up his cross and follow me. What good will it be for a man if he gains the whole world, yet forfeits his soul?"

Jesus (Mt 6:24,26)

The acronym **R.E.D.** can act as a reminder of the three important components of the Red Letter Movement.

Realize the revolution Jesus started and realize that Jesus is calling us to be his revolutionaries in a world of despair.

Engage in the Holy Spirit through spiritual disciplines.

Do the Spirit-filled works of Jesus in our world today.

Realize	*Engage*	*Do*	Impact World
→	→	→	

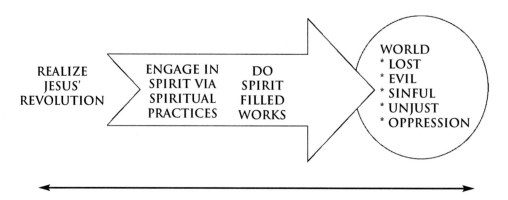

R.E.D. (Realize, Engage and Do) must take place within communitas.

"I glory in Christ Jesus in my service to God. I will not venture to speak of anything except what Christ has accomplished through me in leading the gentiles to obey God by what I have said and done – by the power of signs and miracles, through the power of the Spirit." (Rom 15:17-19)

HOW TO START A RED LETTER MOVEMENT

Here is a practical plan of action for beginning the adventure of the Red Letter Revolution and an outline on how to start up your own Red Letter communitas.

Purpose: To gather regularly as a group of committed Red Letter Christians to worship Jesus, hear his words and fulfill his commands.

1. Make sure every participant can check the following boxes:

❏ **R** – I realize the revolutionary repercussions of the mission of Jesus.

❏ **E** – I will engage in spiritual practices for the filling of the Holy Spirit.

❏ **D** – I will do, in communitas, what God tells me as part of his revolutionary mission.

2. Start off worship by building communitas through sharing a meal together as a group.

Come together like the early Christians did and celebrate the Lord's Supper by actually having a meal together as part of your regular worship. This meal should begin with the breaking of bread and end off with the passing of the cup. In between the formal act of communion, the food should be eaten in a spirit of celebratory joy at what Jesus has done for us on the cross. The participants of the meal can share what God is doing in their lives, encouraging and exhorting one another in their walk with God.

3. Continue worship through a time of singing, prayer and study of the Gospels.

After the meal is done, come together as a group to sing God's praises, share prayer requests and study a Gospel passage with the underlining priority of hearing Jesus tell the group what he wants them to do. Some Red Letter groups find it very helpful to incorporate group lectio divina during the Bible portion of their worship. Whatever method you choose, it is very important to be aware of the following questions to guide your group to action:

A. Key Questions to Ask Based on the Red Letters of Christ
* How do Jesus' red words and actions that we are currently studying impact our world today?
* What do Jesus' red words and actions have to do with politics, war, the environment, poverty, injustice and other realities that we face in our times today?
* What is our responsibility in being involved in fulfilling Jesus' red words and actions by joining God in bringing about his kingdom rule wherever we go?
* Is there something that Jesus wants us to do in light of what we have learned from his red words and actions?

B. Key Questions to Ask Based on the Lord's Prayer (Mt 6:9-13; Lk 11:2-4)
* Is this (social issue) something that happens in the kingdom of God?
"Your kingdom come on earth as it is in heaven."
* Is this (social issue) the will of God?
"Your will be done on earth as it is in heaven."
* Does this (social issue) further the kingdom of God manifesting itself on earth as it is in heaven?

If the answer is no to the above questions, then the issue you are facing is in opposition to the kingdom and will of God and must be confronted.

4. Discuss and commit to any actions that the group feels Jesus wants them to do.

When it is time to finish the Bible study segment of the gathering, spend some quiet time as a group, so that individuals can quietly listen to Jesus to hear if there is any action steps he wants the group to be involved in. After a few minutes of silence, open the floor for more discussion to see if others in the group heard the same message. You will be surprised how uniting these times can be. If there is group consensus to what has been shared, then that is a clear sign to move ahead in making action steps for the group to pursue in obeying Christ. If not, then do not move forward yet.

5. Close the gathering by confirming a time and place for when the next meeting will take place.

A. If the meeting ends with a consensual commitment for revolutionary action:

You now have a central theme for your next meeting. The plan for your group is for each individual to be in prayer and Bible study so that when you gather again you will be set for a plan of action.

B. If the meeting ends without consensual agreement of action:

Continue your next gathering by following steps one to five and allow the Spirit to guide your future meetings.

6. Important extras:

Most Red Letter Christians like to build a monastic rule into their community and mission. This is important, since these rules are foundational practices that enable Red Letter Christians to renounce worldly pursuits in order to fully devote their life to the revolution.

Some groups of Red Letter Christians have committed to living and serving together in intentional community in which they reside together. But most Red Letter Christians do not feel called to actually live together in this form of intimate community. They have discovered that they can still benefit from communal living by setting some form of monastic order to their group without actually living together. This rule of life keeps them focussed on their R.E.D. calling in life.

A good example of this is found in a group of Christians from Australia who call their community "Small Boat Big Sea."[1] These Christians have committed to organize their lives around a simple weekly rhythm known as "B.E.L.L.S." to assist them in being more effective followers of Jesus.

Each letter in the acronym B.E.L.L.S. represents an action they must do each week. The letter B stands for bless, in which they commit to intentionally bless someone through a gift, words of encouragement or another form. E stands for eat and reminds them of their commitment to share a meal or a simple cup of coffee with someone they do not live with. L stands for listening to God at least one day a week through a time of silence or nature walks. The next L in the acronym stands for learn; they commit to study the Scriptures in depth to learn more of God. S stands for sent and encourages them to look for ways they can fulfill the mission of Jesus through their daily activities and individual giftedness.

Each week, members of the Small Boat Big Sea community gather together to share a meal, worship Jesus and encourage each other in their walk with God. They follow the B.E.L.L.S. format during this time of fellowship together. They also have smaller groups of three people that meet weekly to share how their week of B.E.L.L.S. went. This keeps them focused on their weekly rhythm and allows time for prayer and counsel regarding what is happening in their lives. Finally, Small Boat Big Sea also take part in a weekly alternative worship service in which everyone has the opportunity to participate in worshipping God. All of these gatherings are permeated with a desire to hear God's voice, be filled with God's Spirit and to do Jesus' revolutionary work among the poor and oppressed.

There are many ways you can gather together as a Red Letter movement but the key priority is that any gathering must be built on **R.E.D.**—**R**ealizing the revolutionary implications of Jesus and his mission, **E**ngaging in the Spirit through spiritual practices and **D**oing what Jesus tells us through communitas.

NOTES

[1] To learn more about Small Boat Big Sea visit www.smallboatbigsea.org.

BECOMING A FOLLOWER OF CHRIST

We need a Jesus revolution in our world today because we are all guilty of personal sin, as manifested in the corporate evil that we find so despicable. We are not alone in our feelings of disgust. The Bible teaches us that God is holy and pure and because of this, he has to execute justice on all wrongdoing. We deserve God's judgment for our sin, but thank God, he is also all-loving. He sent Jesus to die on the cross as an incredible act of grace to our distressed souls and troubled world. Jesus paid the price for our sin by taking the judgment of God we deserved, and he offers his forgiveness to us today. All we have to do is ask Jesus to forgive us of our sin and to be the Saviour and Lord of our lives. When this happens, Jesus revolutionizes you so that you can revolutionize the world.

If you have never asked Jesus to forgive you of your sin, do so now. Say this prayer sincerely: "Jesus, I am a sinner. I recognize that the evil in this world is also in me. Thank you for dying on the cross for me. Please forgive me of my sin. Enter into my life as Lord and allow me to follow you the rest of the days of my life as a Red Letter Revolutionary. Amen."

If you said this prayer, please take a look at the passage below from "The Message" version of the Bible. It explains everything Jesus has done for you and our world:

> The God-setting-things-right that we read about has become Jesus-setting-things-right for us. And not only for us, but for

everyone who believes in him…Since we've compiled this long and sorry record as sinners and proved that we are utterly incapable of living the glorious lives God wills for us, God did it for us. Out of sheer generosity, he put us in right standing with himself. A pure gift. He got us out of the mess we're in and restored us to where he always wanted us to be. And he did it by means of Jesus Christ. God sacrificed Jesus on the altar of the world to clear that world of sin. Having faith in him sets us in the clear. God decided on this course of action in full view of the public—to set the world in the clear with himself through the sacrifice of Jesus, finally taking care of the sins he had so patiently endured. This is not only clear, but it's now—this is current history! God sets things right. He also makes it possible for us to live in his rightness. (Rom 3:22-26, *The Message Bible*)

Now join the Red Letter Movement by **R**ecognizing the revolutionary implications of Jesus by reading the gospels of Christ. **E**ngage your soul in his Holy Spirit through spiritual practices. **D**o his revolutionary work in this world by joining a group of like-minded Red Letter Christians.

THE RED LETTER REVOLUTION MOVEMENT

Looking to join the Red Letter Revolution movement? Here are a few good starting points to consider.

UrbanPromise Toronto - www.urbanpromise.com

If you are interested in the ministry that I work for, then visit www.urbanpromise.com for more information. This website will guide you through various ways you can be involved in urban ministry in cities like Toronto, Ontario; Camden, New Jersey; Wilmington, Delaware; and Vancouver, British Columbia. There are also new UrbanPromise sites being developed in Africa and South America.

World Vision - www.worldvision.ca

My friends at World Vision Canada are among the top in their field when it comes to meeting the needs of the world's poorest populations. Please click onto their website at www.worldvision.ca to discover various ways you can join them in the vital work they do on behalf of the poor.

Dr. Tony Campolo / EAPE - www.tonycampolo.org

My good friend Dr. Tony Campolo and his ministry Evangelical Association for the Promotion of Education (EAPE) have formed a key Christian voice on behalf of the poor and oppressed for years. To learn more about the many Red Letter causes he is involved with, including a treasure trove of great resources, visit his website, www.tonycampolo.org.

Speaking - www.urbanpromise.com

I am available to speak at corporate, church or other functions. To make a booking, download the speaker request form on UrbanPromise Toronto's website at www.urbanpromise.com. Or, you can contact me at:

UrbanPromise Toronto
364 Old Kingston Rd. P.O. Box 97512
M1C 4Z1
Scarborough, Ontario
Canada
(416) 516-6121 ext. 21

ALSO BY COLIN McCARTNEY

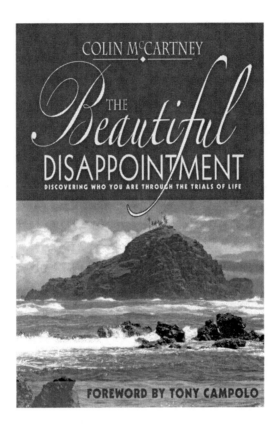

www.castlequaybooks.com

CASTLE QUAY BOOKS

OTHER CASTLE QUAY TITLES INCLUDE:
Walking Towards Hope
The Chicago Healer
Seven Angels for Seven Days
Making Your Dreams Your Destiny
The Way They Should Go
The Defilers
Jesus and Caesar
Jason Has Been Shot!
The Cardboard Shack Beneath the Bridge
Keep On Standing - **NEW!**
To My Family - **NEW!**
Through Fire & Sea
One Smooth Stone
Vision that Works - **NEW!**
The Beautiful Disappointment - **NEW!**
Bent Hope - **NEW!**

BAYRIDGE BOOKS TITLES:
Counterfeit Code: Answering The Da Vinci Code Heresies
Wars Are Never Enough: The Joao Matwawana Story
More Faithful Than We Think
Save My Children - **NEW!**
What the Preacher Forgot to Tell Me - **NEW!**
*To Be Continued: The Story of the Salvation Army
in Woodstock* - **NEW!**

For more information and to explore the rest of our titles visit
www.castlequaybooks.com